Praise of Purpo

As the title might suggest, this is a book about individual people, but the principles it contains apply to all. Each chapter comes from a different contributor with their own area of expertise, but the end result is a sum that is so much greater than the parts. There are lessons in leadership, lessons in life, and strong messages aplenty from individuals who have experienced both triumph and adversity. The end result is a series of essays that stitch into a powerful tapestry, a compelling picture of leading and prevailing in the world we live in today. - and the subtle progression of knowledge as you read on - is the real reward. A delight. **- Monty Halls - Travel Writer, Broadcaster, Marine Biologist, Inspirational Speaker, Leadership Trainer, Expedition Leader**

This book is jammed packed with real-world experience. It is full of practice from the mouth of leaders who have done it. 20 different perspectives on delivering profound change that share personal truths and harsh realities. This collection of insights is fascinating, seeing how others have followed their purpose will inspire you to find yours. **- Gavin Bounds Chief Operating Officer EMEA. Rackspace Chair PurpleSpace**

Purposeful People is a simply amazing display of practical advices and metaphors from a wide array of leaders, compiled by Chris Paton, is meant for leaders who want to become better selves, and leap from Good to Great. The best leadership guide in years. **- Joao Perez, Senior Vice President, Oracle**

One of the best books I have read in leadership in years and I strongly recommend any leaders who want to master this approach & how to create a valuable framework that integrates purpose, values and goals read it. **- Glenn Marsden, CEO & Founder; Imperfectly Perfect Campaign**

Purposeful People - what an understated title! This compilation is packed with excellence, learning and experience from real leaders who have really walked the walk.

There is so much content and knowledge share - Leadership, teams, values, decision making, organisational development, inclusivity, the formula for innovation (!) self growth from several angles, work / life blend and even sleep! I am sure there will be something for everyone within the pages, dig in and learn.

The authors have included references, further reading, podcasts, TED talks and contacts to enable the reader to delve deeper and further beyond the book and continue the life long learning journey. **- Conrad Trickett, Chief Superintendent, Divisional Commander, Highland & Islands Division, Police Scotland**

Whether new in post or experienced, there will be something for you. A recommended read for anyone with positive enquiry and a growth mindset. **- Phil Jones MBE**

I admit I'm suspicious of business books, especially those written by academics and researchers. This is snooty of me I know, but I trust practice over theory any day.

That's where this book scores high. The writers are all practitioners, which means these ideas have been fashioned at the coal-face, not in a library or by studying other people's work.

There's a great deal of practical business humanity to learn in these pages, much of it that you won't find anywhere else. **- Richard Eyre CBE, Formerly CEO of ITV and Chairman of the Eden Project**

"An encyclopaedia of life, a book of knowledge, a compendium of wisdom, I am lost in my ability to describe 'Purposeful People', it is an amazing amalgam of experience, success, opportunity, setback, bounce back and fortitude.

Thank you, thank you, thank you, to all those who have contributed to this invaluable book, 'Purposeful People' is my new bible! **- Nicholas Watkins, Principal Q4 Management Limited**

Its force rests with the collage of wisdom it provides and its invitation for you to assimilate and apply that within your own purposeful life. **- Patrick Aylward, Collaborative Paths, www.collaborativepath.ca**

'Purposeful People' is a trove of valuable life lessons from a selection of those who truly breathe purpose and as a result, have enjoyed huge success and professional fulfilment. The book is a positive, refreshing concentrate, with no watering down. I felt like each chapter could have been a whole book, but given my time-poor life I'm so grateful the insights were condensed in this way: colourful, engaging, personal stories interwoven with highly actionable take-aways. This is definitely a book to first devour and then keep close at hand for dipping back into at appropriate moments when seeking both inspiration and tangible techniques to not only help us identify but to realise our very individual purpose in life. **- Jess Butcher MBE (Entrepreneur, advisor, equalities commissioner)**

The book describes a roadmap to recovery and a claw back from difficult situations: financial, emotional, and reputational, to name but a few.

No matter what your background, you can relate and see yourself in the lives of many of these authors, these purposeful people from whom you may get guidance to define your direction and purpose in life. **- Professor Sir Keith Porter, Professor of Clinical Traumatology, O St J MD MBBS FRCS(Eng) FRCS(Ed) FIMC RCS(ED) FFSEM(Ed) FCEM FRSA FRCGP(Hon)**

This book provides thought-provoking, inspirational and practical insights to help you move forward faster and enjoy more fulfilment in life. **- Dr Arnoud Franken, Senior Strategy & Change Consultant at InContext Consultancy Group (NL) and Visiting Senior Lecturer at Cranfield University (UK).**

This powerful collection of actionable insights and practical advice from twenty renowned leaders will be a ready companion to me for many years. **- Colonel (Ret) Chris Kolenda, Strategic Leaders Academy**

As someone who has been on a journey to live a meaningful and purposeful life over the past few years, 'Purposeful People' couldn't have come at a better time. It is basically a consolidation of all the advice I have needed.

The book is well laid out, with the topics sequenced in such a way that the reader can choose to read from cover to cover, or can simply select the topics of interest. **- Willorna Brock Chartered MCIPD, HR Consultant, Career and Executive Coach**

The messages imparted by these authors, and the self-reflection they inspire, helped me to address unfamiliar and complex leadership challenges, and I am convinced that not only will this book help others in my profession, but that I will revisit different chapters at different points in my own career. **- Dr Catriona Middleton MRCPCH MBChB BScHons PGCert**

This book is simple, straightforward and digestible. It's a treasure chest of insights that make you stop and think very carefully. The lessons give us a valuable checklist of things that we can all try, test and learn from when put into action (go do it!). I consider this to be a handbook to help us humans navigate the ever-growing societal changes and economic forces around us. **- Melanie Fitzpatrick, Chief People & Brand Officer, CPA Global, Clarivate Plc. BA (hons), Post Grad Diploma (PGDip), Chartered Institute of Marketing, Diploma Marketing (DipM), Market Research Society Diploma (DipMRS)**

It's unusual to find a book that's something for everyone. A book that's insightful, passionate, technical yet compassionate. 'Purposeful People' tells real people's stories of challenges, failures, successes and their deep learning on those journeys. Well worth a read and a book that you will keep coming back to. **- Fraser Morrison, CEO of the 1000 Steps business growth consultancy, and world-ranked endurance athlete.**

Each chapter of this thoughtful and thought-provoking compilation tells its own self-contained story, penned by people from all walks of life. I enjoyed meeting every one of them and contemplating their honest accounts of success, failure and fulfilment in business and in life.

My advice before you dive into these pages – take your time. Each contribution is distinctive and worth digesting. Stew on it a bit before chasing the next nugget. **- Kathryn McKee, Chart MCIPR, head of communications, bp scotland**

PURPOSEFUL PEOPLE

COMPILED BY CHRIS PATON

BOOKS

A catalogue record for this
work is available from the
National Library of Australia

National Library of Australia Catalogue-in-Publication data:
Purposeful People/Chris Paton

ISBN: 978-0-6450520-5-3
(Paperback)

ISBN: 978-0-6451353-0-5
(eBook)

Contents

Working smart is, of course, the ideal scenario. Working hard should be a 'given.' If you do not have a work ethic, if you do not give 100%, then don't expect to get as lucky as I have been.

1

ANDREW POWELL
SELF BELIEF
The boy from nowhere!
(And five key lessons)

Welcome to a book that will help shape the rest of your lives. The authors that I am so privileged to be working alongside have so many gifts to give you along the journey ahead, so do indulge yourself!

So, welcome to Chapter One and let's make a start.

Most stories start at the beginning and end, at the end. So, let's not do that. Let's start this book a little differently with coming right forward to today.

It is 2021 and I am lucky enough to be the founder of the route2work group. A group of companies that together places north of 5000 talented people into work-based opportunity every year through the provision of vocational educational programmes that lead to employment. Many of these talented people come from socially deprived and disadvantaged backgrounds and go on to achieve amazing careers and lives for themselves as a result of our business interventions.

I am genuinely living my dream, following my passion and making a difference.

So, now you know where I am today, let us go back to the very beginning and share with you the story of how I arrived here. You may find that our stories are not that different…

It is 1978 and I am nine years old, living on one of the most run-down estates in South Wales. Home was a block of flats that had been condemned by the local council. I suppose you could describe me as a 'feral child'. A fighter, a thief, unruly, but with a strong work ethic and maybe also a little bit of 'budding entrepreneur.'

Dad worked for thirty-five years in the Ford Motor Company; doing the same job, six days a week, twelve-hour shifts. Mum was the family rock; a tough disciplinarian who liked to party, drink and have the odd fist-fight. She didn't care if it was with a man or a woman; nobody messed with my Mam.

My daily routine, from eight years of age, was to get my backside out of bed at 5am, meet 'John the Milk', our local milkman, to deliver milk, bread and potatoes to the whole estate, up and down six flights of stairs, across eighteen blocks, for two and a half hours every weekday and Saturday morning. John was smart. He read his Sun newspaper and smoked his fags, as I did his job, for fifty pence a week!

Thursday night, bi-weekly, was where I earned some serious money. A whole pound!

Picked up from the estate with a few other kids, we would be taken around local scrap yards, with a list of parts to steal to order, for a notorious local scrap merchant. Friday afternoons, post our raids, we would bunk off school and head to an 'off the beaten track' pub, where the unnamed notorious scrap dealer would treat us kids to a pint of raw cider in a back room, out of sight of the other drinkers. Think Fagan and Oliver Twist!

Sport was my escape. I loved my football, rugby, and boxing, and I was pretty decent at all three, even at that tender age. I played football to county standard, played for the best under-10 club team in the region, and was team and county captain. My downfall, I liked a fight a little too much.

Then life changed. My fighting got the attention of the local police after an incident that saw me beat up on an Irish lad from the estate, and in the process unintentionally hurt his sister. It was serious.

The police, un-uniformed, turned up at the flat door to talk to my parents. A young offenders institute was mentioned as an option.

My parents knew that my path ahead was littered with danger if they did not change my environment. Somehow they secured a house move into a suburban area; it was less than a mile away but removed me from the immediate troubles of the flats.

Work ethic still intact, I convinced the local newsagent to take me on as a paperboy. I had two paper rounds that paid me £5.35 a week. That was a lot of money back then for a nine-year-old.

What happened, as I settled into my new home, new school, new friends, is that I had been taken out of a specific environment and been given a chance. I no longer had a desire to thieve for the local scrap merchant. I no longer needed to prove my place in the pecking order on a tough council estate.

Fast forward a few years. At fifteen I was playing football to a very high standard, and I had a few trials with some professional clubs to become an apprentice footballer. I didn't make it! I wasn't good enough! My future looked like a choice between a good, honest career working in a factory like my Dad, unemployment, or to revert back to my old ways, leading inevitably to prison at some point. My parents could never afford to send me through to higher education. So, what was I to do?

I wanted my world to be bigger than the Severn Bridge toll barrier, so I popped off to the Army Careers Office in Swansea and took a written entry test. I didn't tell my parents. I failed! I wanted a trade; I didn't want to join the infantry. No disrespect, the infantry does an amazing job, but it just wasn't for me.

Six weeks later, I was back in that Army careers office in Swansea, with a second bash at the entry test. I passed! I could now choose a career as an engineer, either in the Royal Signals or the Royal Engineers. I asked which of the two jobs started first. It was that simple, no thought behind the choice. I told my parents. Initially horrified, they eventually signed the consent forms. I joined the Army Apprentices College in Harrogate, aged sixteen. I was to train to become an Electronic Engineer.

Let us take a moment to pause here. Thus far you have been reading the journey of a young man who seems to have been very lucky and who seems to have avoided car crash scenarios by the skin of his pants, and you would be right! Sure, I made some smart choices, sure I believed enough in myself to not conform to the norm, and yes I must have had some talent, but I also had luck. Lots of luck!

LESSON ONE: THE HARDER I TRIED, THE HARDER I WORKED, THE LUCKIER I GOT.

Working smart is, of course, the ideal scenario. Working hard should be a 'given.' If you do not have a work ethic, if you do not give 100%, then don't expect to get as lucky as I have been.

The Army was a breeze for me. Yes, I initially missed home, but I had found my niche. The military taught me self-discipline, how to look after myself, it gave me leadership opportunities and threw as much sport at me as

I could handle. I excelled. I became captain of the Army junior football team and I boxed and played rugby for the College.

I graduated Harrogate as a boy Sergeant Major. I then went off to Catterick Garrison to complete my trade training prior to being posted to the Royal School of Signals in Blandford Forum (they were the Army football champions).

Two years into my time at Blandford and edging toward my 20th Birthday, I was bored! All I seemed to do was play sport, drink beer, and do the odd technical data installation with my team. I went to see my Commanding Officer to talk about what the Army could throw at me. He talked to me intoxicatingly about some mysterious men who were the elite of the elite, in a far-off place called Stirling Lines in Hereford. He caveated the conversation by explicitly telling me that while this would be the most significant challenge the British Army could throw at me, I had no chance of ever going there. Unfortunately, from his perspective, I was a lazy footballer, with no military skills to speak of. Someone say 'red rag to a bull?'

I trained my backside off over the next few months and rocked up at Stirling Lines in Hereford in purple jeans and earrings. The gate guard pulled me into his office, forced me to get out of the said jeans and take my earrings out, and with a laugh and a shake of his head, sent me into the barracks.

Fast forward several months and I had passed Special Forces selection. I was battered, bruised, had no toenails, had lost a few stone in weight and had seen many men better, fitter and smarter than me, not make it. I was now a Special Forces soldier.

My career at Hereford saw me serve in the Gulf, the former Yugoslavia, Northern Ireland, and across a few other global locations that should not be shared here.

The military enabled me to see humanity at its best, and unfortunately, at its worst. It taught me many life lessons that I have brought into my business career and that I hope have helped to shape the leader I am today.

LESSON TWO: NEVER EVER LET ANYONE TELL YOU THAT YOU CANNOT ACHIEVE SOMETHING.

You are unique! You are you! Take control of your life and make your own choices!

Don't let Mum, Dad, Auntie, Uncle, Granny, Grandad, your boss, or your Commanding Officer, tell you the limit of your potential based on their own knowledge, history, failings, and conditioning.

Only you can determine what you are capable of. Only you can decide how deep you want to dig to build the life you want and deserve.

I left the military in 1996. I was twenty-seven years old. I had two beautiful children (girls, Brogan & Morgan), a failing marriage (mostly my fault for being away so much whilst at Hereford), and I had no idea what civilian life had to offer me. I had been conditioned from the age of sixteen to behave in very clear ways; to react to scenarios and to engage life with a dark humour driven by experiences across an eleven-year military career. How would I cope?

My first civilian role was in a Telecoms department at a Financial Services business, in Basingstoke. My boss was a great guy. His brother and father were both ex-military so he 'got me.' The team was also awesome and I settled very quickly, with a few erm…faux pas, relating to corporate etiquette. I also got divorced and suffered a little with what is now known as PTSD.

My career post this was a mixture of walking into businesses that were growing so fast that they were in a state of complete disorganisation, and companies that were in the financial crap. Both scenarios enabled me to bring my skillset to the fore, to excel, and to take on wider and more significant leadership roles. In parallel, I had met Sally, my now wife, and life partner.

LESSON THREE: CHANGE IS A CONSTANT. DON'T TRY AND FIGHT IT. IT IS HAPPENING EVERY DAY AND ALL AROUND US. THE MINUTE YOU STAND STILL, YOU BECOME OBSOLETE.

What I have not shared is that I built a company and lost everything. I have experienced crap bosses who couldn't lead their way out of a paper bag, and I have made many mistakes, some of them huge. But I have not let anything define me. I can't change history. I can only learn from it.

The pinnacle of my then career came when I joined City of London Telecom (COLT). I found a CEO and leader who saw my raw talent, who understood my value set and my leadership potential, and who threw me into the deep end across multiple roles and multiple scenarios. I found myself in the right place, at the right time, with a leader who believed in me. I got lucky again!

This is where I started to hone my leadership style to fit the corporate world. All of the lessons I learned from my military career seeing 'leadership as a service', and treating the janitor and receptionist with as much due care and attention as my fellow executives, all came together for me.

I ended my time at COLT as Global Chief Operating Officer (COO), of a FTSE 250 business. I was super proud.

LESSON FOUR: DO NOT SET YOURSELF BOUNDARIES ON WHAT YOU THINK YOU ARE CAPABLE OF. YOU MAY SURPRISE YOURSELF.

Do you think you would fail if you were thrown into a major leadership role tomorrow? How would you know? Grasp every opportunity. Open every door. Trust yourself to learn as you go and if you fail…well, how do you measure failure? If you are perceived to fail, or you feel you have failed, it is a moment in time. Reflect, learn, get off your ass, and go again.

I left COLT not because I had to, but because I chose to. I had a new young family; a son of ten, Dylan, a daughter of seven, Erin, and Brogan and Morgan from my first marriage, who were now 20 and 18 respectively. I had spent my six years at COLT on a plane. The military had taught me that real leadership meant; 'being present,' yet my family had come second, again! I wasn't learning from my mistakes and I was about to miss out on my second family growing up, right in front of me.

I resigned with no job to go to. No new salary awaiting. No security. But I trusted myself. I believed in myself, and I knew the right thing would come along.

My life now needed a purpose. My next professional challenge needed to light something within me. I wanted to do something to change people's lives.

My salvation was a little business in Poole. It was perfect. It took predominantly inner city, disadvantaged adults, trained them to become personal trainers, and gave them access to careers in gyms all across the UK. Perfect!

An hour's drive from home, a business with a purpose, an operating model I could scale, and an opportunity to change people's lives; people who were just like the fifteen-year-old me.

Fast forward six years and that little business is now the route2work group. We are changing the world of education and careers, one step at a time. I have found my passion. We are changing people's lives.

LESSON FIVE: DON'T JUST DO A JOB! LIFE IS FAR TOO SHORT TO NOT BE DOING SOMETHING YOU LOVE AND ARE PASSIONATE ABOUT.

'Easy for you to say,' I hear you proclaim. Not really. I am genuinely a boy from nowhere. I have travelled the world, served in conflicts, sat on the executive teams of global businesses, chaired boards, and I am now changing lives. The boy from a council estate - if I can do it, why can't you? Sure, I had some luck. Sure, I was in the right place at the right time on occasion, but it can't be all down to luck!

So, stop feeling sorry for yourself; stop worrying about poor choices you have made, or worrying about your perceived historic failures. You can't change any of that, but you can learn from it.

You can get up off the canvas and ensure that the rest of your life is filled with purpose, making conscious choices about how you spend your days, about what you contribute to society, about how you nurture and love those who are precious to you. Life is now a promising array of choices that you can consciously consider and revel in, and I wish you luck!

I do hope this brief engagement has been of value, and that I have lit a small fire for you. A fire that will now burn and gather intensity as you fuel yourself with knowledge, tools, and techniques from this book that will enable a 'better equipped, more resilient, passionate and self-believing you' to emerge.

I leave you with my favourite mantra:

'Talent develops in quiet places, our challenge as leaders is to find it!'

Have fun. Life is far too short!

A SHORT REMINDER OF THE FIVE LESSONS:

1. The harder you try, the harder you work, the luckier you will get
2. Never ever let anyone tell you that you cannot achieve something
3. Change is a constant. Embrace it, learn how to navigate your way across it, make it work for you
4. Do not set yourself boundaries on what you think you are capable of. You will surprise yourself
5. Don't just do a job! Life is far too short to not be doing something that you love and are passionate about

ABOUT THE AUTHOR

Andrew hails from humble beginnings on one of the most run-down council estates in South Wales. https://www.youtube.com/watch?v=Fgwbn5IyVs4

This start in life instilled into Andrew a voracious will to win, which manifested itself on the football & rugby field, in the boxing ring and later in military life and on into business.

An ex-soldier who served his country proudly from the age of sixteen, he served for eleven years across many continents, a few conflicts and with the UK Special Forces for over five years.

He remains a keen advocate of supporting ex-forces talent and works extremely hard, wherever possible, to support this talent to make seamless transitions into civilian life and meaningful employment-based opportunities.

His business journey has enabled him to operate globally, including spending six years at recently privatised FTSE 250 company: Colt Technology Services, where he served in leadership roles across several executive functions, ending as Group Chief Operating Officer and with a place on operating Boards as Chairman of many of its country subsidiaries.

He has found a passion for 'levelling the playing field' for talent by providing educational programmes that lead to employment-based opportunity using amazing technology provision, and as a result, the opportunity to create a positive social impact.

Andrew is the Founder and a Director of the route2work group. www.route2work.com (R2W)

R2W is a careers development company that connects people to opportunity through a technology driven ECOSYSTEM. This system encompasses: attraction, assessment, training, graduation and placement into industry through established employer partnerships.

The business develops pipelines of talent and career pathways into its target sectors, focusing on market dynamics where skills gaps exist or are emerging.

Through thinking differently, R2W unlocks hidden talent that traditionally has faced barriers to entry into aspirational careers, with a specific focus on social mobility and the diversity & inclusion agendas.

The group has placed over 12,000 talented people into career-based opportunities across the UK through vendor or industry standard educational and qualification-based programmes since 2017. The group operates two companies: www.thetrainingroom.com & www.infinityglobal.io

Across the R2W journey Andrew has raised more than £10m in new investment to help fund the social impact mission he is on. He has been shortlisted in 2021 as a finalist at the Armed Forces in Business Awards in the category: "Entrepreneur of the year".

Andrew is also a charity champion for Dreams Come True: https://www.dreamscometrue.uk.com a charity that focuses on making individual dreams a reality for terminally ill or seriously life impaired children, and over the past ten years, with his wife Sally, he has raised more than £50k through many differing events, including running marathons and organising and hosting charity tribute nights and gala balls.

As a leader, he has a favourite mantra: "talent develops in quiet places, our challenge is to find it."

Finding purpose doesn't always come from a singular event. For many of us it can take a number of years and searching within before becoming clear on what impact we want to make in the world.

2

SARAH DOWNS
THE ROAD TO FINDING YOUR PURPOSE

INTRODUCTION

I was 9 years old. It was a cold Saturday morning, and I was at the local nursing home where my mum worked. It was the annual Christmas bake sale which Mum took me and my sister to every year, but this one was different, and I wouldn't realise the significance of it for many years. I was sat on a sofa, positioned directly in front of a large bay window overlooking the coast of our seaside hometown. My legs were swinging back and forth as they were much too short to reach the floor, and I could never sit still as a child. My younger sister sat beside me eating cake and looking around the room, wide-eyed at all the goings-on. Carers were busy navigating the residents to their armchairs and serving refreshments.

I was distracted by the seagull sitting on the outside windowsill when I heard a loud cry which made me jump. The man in the navy jumper sitting across from us looked terrified and had started shouting at everyone around him while banging his cup on the table. Only a few minutes before he had been asleep and I had been observing his glasses sliding down his long nose, wondering if they'd fall off. I was too young to understand at the time, but the man was likely suffering from either Dementia or Alzheimer's disease.

I watched closely as Mum walked towards the man with a kind smile on her face. Mum sat beside him and held his hand. I couldn't hear the words coming from her mouth, but I could tell by the man's reaction that they were soothing. Within a matter of minutes, he was smiling and laughing at something my mum had said. Another carer arrived with a cup of tea and a plate of sweet treats. The drama was over.

When I remember that moment, it's as if it happened yesterday. It was the first time I was aware of being inspired by something. I was inspired by my mum and her actions. I wanted to make things better the way she did. I wanted to help people. Had I found my purpose? It was certainly the start of my journey.

FINDING PURPOSE IN LIFE

Finding purpose doesn't always come from a singular event. For many of us it can take a number of years and searching within before becoming clear on what impact we want to make in the world. Personally, I went through a traumatic event followed by some health issues throughout my teenage years, which pulled me closer to where I was headed. I felt a deep sense of gratitude every time someone helped me; whether that be my parents, teachers, the doctors or the psychologist that supported me to deal with PTSD. By the time I was ready to go into higher education, I was clear that I wanted to care for others and make a difference in someone's life. I just wasn't sure of the 'what' or the 'how.'

Many years later, I arrived on the ward ready for the nightshift handover. I worked in the local trauma unit so there was always a lot going on. Long shifts full of anxiety, relief, adrenaline, tears and laughter. We did what we needed to do, and tried our best to pull each other through the worst of it. I never knew what I was walking into, as each and every shift brought something new: a different set of challenges, a medical condition I'd never heard of before, people from all walks of life and in need of various levels of care. This night was going to be tough and one I'd remember forever.

I had dealt with many deaths and even though they were all hard, I knew I could cope. Now and again I was involved with a case that ingrained a little deeper. As each one presented a different set of circumstances, I wasn't sure why, but some definitely affected me more than others. Often the deaths I remember in detail were traumatic and sometimes almost surreal, but tonight was different.

I had nursed Mary for many months; she was nearing 100 years old and had a wicked sense of humour, which kept us nurses on our toes. She also liked to take a swipe at the doctors who had poor bedside manner. I had sat with Mary only 4 days before talking about her favourite pastime: The Jeremy Kyle Show, a TV programme I personally couldn't stand to watch, but I enjoyed her re-enactment of it. There were things spoken about on the show that a woman of her age struggled to comprehend, which filled her with amazement and questions for us 'young ones.' Mary would often start her sentences with 'back in my day,' which always alerted us that she had a lesson in store.

During handover, my nurse manager advised us that Mary was deteriorating quickly and suggested that we keep a close eye on her overnight. I offered to sit with Mary as we had enough staff on duty that evening to cover the ward. I took a deep breath before entering her room, with a hint of anxiety, uncertain of what would be on the other side. Mary was asleep in the dimly lit room but woke shortly after to ask for some water. Every request from Mary came with a big smile and twinkling eyes. She sighed and sunk back into her pillow after her drink. She was weak, tired and not the same lively lady I remembered from only days before.

I gave her a wash and changed her nightgown to settle her for the night. Mary often spoke of her love for a warm facecloth against her skin and even on this night, as she lay there with closed eyes and she smiled as I bathed her hands and face. Simple things. Mary fell into a deep sleep, wrapped up in bedding with her favourite knitted blanket on top; a gift from a friend in her nursing home. It was multi-coloured and had little embroidered flowers around the edges. That night I counted 64 flowers while sitting and waiting with her, trying to stay focussed on her every move and breath, looking for signs that she may need something more to keep her comfortable. Mary woke every couple of hours for a drink or to ask the time. On one occasion she told me off for still being by her side, as she didn't want to be a 'nuisance.' I held her hand, which felt small and delicate, the skin thinned from old age. Mary was warm to touch but her hands had become cold. I tucked them under the blanket and placed my own hand on her arm, moving my fingers gently so she could feel them. A small gesture to let her know I was there.

The hours dragged by. I could hear the hustle and bustle of the busy ward outside the closed door, footsteps, talking, machines pinging and buzzers ringing. But it wasn't enough to distract me as I had an important job to do and I needed to be completely present. By 5am that morning, Mary had passed away, comfortable and asleep, the way most of us hope it will happen when it's our time. I felt a mix of emotions. I was sad that she was no longer there knowing that she would be missed by everyone who knew her, but also relieved that she had experienced a peaceful death with an awareness that someone was by her side. I felt privileged and grateful that I was able to be with her at the end. I knew that it would continue to be difficult but I was absolutely sure that this was what I was meant to be doing…I was fulfilling my life's purpose.

I'm often asked how to find purpose in life. This question used to confuse me as I had found my own fairly organically, albeit not straightforward. I was one of the lucky ones. My purpose had come to me rather than me needing to search. From childhood I had started to create my own recipe without even realising it. Like many homemade recipes, it only gets better with time, with a little trial and error sprinkled on top. I've thought about this long and hard and I will leave you with some questions to ponder.

1. When you are no longer here, what do you want people to say about you?
2. What is the ONE ingredient you'd always know was missing?
3. What makes you feel fulfilled?
4. What do you want to achieve each day, even the little things?

Some of these can be hard to answer for someone who hasn't yet found their purpose. People often jump to answers they assume others will expect from them, but are they being true to themselves? A mentor of mine once said that finding your purpose is like being stuck in a library for a few weeks. You're given enough food and water to see you through, but you have nothing else to occupy your time but the books on the many shelves. Sounds great, right? Think about what genres you would go to first. There may be one or many and there is no right or wrong answer. Identifying what you care about, what excites you, and what you want to personally develop in can help you to go deep on finding purpose.

CAN WE LOSE OUR PURPOSE?

After 5 years on the trauma ward, I was diagnosed with epilepsy. The result: I had to leave my career which was never part of my plan. I had to find a job that wouldn't put others in harm's way if I collapsed and started to seizure. I had gone from helping people to being a risk to them. I was devastated and struggled to see how I would find purpose in any other career. My confidence was knocked with each and every job application. At recruitment agencies I was told, 'I don't know what to do with you. You're a nurse. Sorry.' Not once were transferable skills mentioned.

When I started my first job in the world of business, I felt like I was standing at the foot of a mountain. I had so much to learn and knew it was going to take a long time and a lot of energy to get anywhere close to the top. I had built a lot of resilience over the years. I knew if I put my mind to it I would get there and I would be fine, but if I'm honest, I was dreading the journey.

Luckily, I ended up working for a director who could see my transferable skills and mentored me on an almost daily basis, to ensure I developed and achieved in the role. She had identified that I could handle almost anything she would throw at me based on my answer to the popular interview question, 'When have you had to overcome a challenge in the workplace, and how did you handle it?' I had responded, 'I've been a trauma nurse working in a life-or-death environment. I just had to get on with it. Some days were harder than others, but we all had an important job to do and that came first.' When I asked a year later, I was told that was the main reason I got the job.

Within a few months of starting my new role, I was aware that something was missing. I liked the people I worked with and the tasks weren't awful, but I just felt a gaping hole inside. I realised I was no longer doing something that aligned with my purpose. Something had to change. I volunteered for a number of charities and started studying to work on my personal development. I could already see that there were plenty of people to help in business, but that it would be easier to make an impact the closer I got to the top.

Within a few years, I set up my own consultancy, working with leadership teams on their strategic objectives. My focus was on revenue growth and the performance of their people; to make sure that all moving parts were working well together and they met their business goals. I had realised working as an employee for a few companies and networking with others, that management teams were quick to jump into 'surgery,' requesting new processes, systems, training and recruitment etc. But like in medicine, you should never jump into the surgery before running the right diagnostic tests. I decided to work on my own and help management do the MRI so that the treatment plan would be exactly what was required. What I hadn't realised at this point was how close I would get to the CEOs and MDs. I never thought they would let me in and talk to me about their own symptoms, as well as the businesses they were running. I now understand that the two are closely connected, but that took time.

I had a client, and to protect his identity, I will call him George. He was the founder of a technology business that had just celebrated a large contract win. On the face of it, the business was doing well. But George had fallen out of love with it; 'It used to be my baby but I'm not sure I like what it's grown into,' he said. I remember one meeting in particular where George was very emotional and told me he was ready to give up. All the experience I had, working with people in both physical and mental pain rushed back, and I supported him through it step by step. A few months later he thanked me and told me that he felt excited about his future and what he wanted to achieve with the business. It felt familiar and comfortable, which was unrecognisable in the moment, but I soon realised I was feeling something that I hadn't felt for a long time. I was helping, truly helping. I was making a difference to someone's life, just in a different way. That was the moment I realised there were ways to fulfil my purpose and help others, without a career in nursing. There were times in my business life where I felt I'd lost my purpose, but I realised there are many roads to a single destination, and I just needed to turn right at the crossroads.

'Leadership is about empathy. It is about having the ability to relate and to connect with people for the purpose of inspiring and empowering their lives.' - Daniel H. Pink

THE NEXT CHAPTER

It's been a long road so far and I'm still on the journey. It's taken a great deal of strength and the resilience I've built over time has most certainly helped. I've made mistakes and learned from them. From my experience in trauma nursing, I'm used to working under pressure but sometimes still don't make the right decisions. With continuous development, I'm confident of finding new ways to fulfil my life's purpose – to help others in any way I can.

ABOUT THE AUTHOR

With many years working as a nurse, mostly in Trauma Orthopaedics, Sarah is no stranger to working under pressure. She is an excellent listener and has the ability to build trust in relationships and lead people in a fast-paced environment. While actively listening and using her empathy and compassion, her nursing experience now assists her work with business clients to achieve their objectives, by focusing on strategy and creating positive collaborations.

After an epilepsy diagnosis in 2011, Sarah left the healthcare sector to start her business career. Without knowing where she would fit in, her journey was to find a role that aligned with her purpose; drawing on her experience in communication, strategy and leadership, as well as her life lessons in navigating uncertainty, building resilience and working with individuals on a personal level.

As an entrepreneur, Sarah has a passion for sales, which has resulted in her founding 2 consultancy businesses over recent years. She is now working full-time in Doqaru Ltd, where she is the Co-Founding Director. She teaches her clients to 'sell like a nurse' by utilising the processes and techniques she gained from her transferable skills. By starting with the MRI instead of jumping into the surgery, she works with CEOs to understand what is really going on in their organisations using data-driven insights. She has helped businesses from Start-up to Fortune 500, to start-up, grow, exit and diversify in industries such as Technology, Oil & Gas, Offshore Renewables, Nuclear and Professional Services.

Sarah is passionate about people and believes in giving back. She has been involved with a number of Third Sector organisations as a volunteer, advisor and non-executive director. She is an advocate for Mental Health and supports Domestic Violence campaigns. Sarah also spends her time mentoring Young Professionals and Start-Up founders.

Outside of work, Sarah enjoys spending time outdoors with her family, including her 4-year old son Jacob; living on the coastline of the North-East of Scotland, there are endless walks and castles to explore. She also enjoys trying new Scottish craft gins when she gets the opportunity.

Use your gut. Not the 'lucky guess' intuition though, but informed intuition. 'Informed Intuition' is developed over a period of time and is largely shaped by your past experiences and knowledge.

COLM GAYTON

3 DECISION MAKING AND STRESS

1. INTRODUCTION

I make decisions every day – some good and, certainly sometimes, bad. Everybody does. Decision-making is like breathing. We do it on occasions, without thinking (habitual decisions) and sometimes, we really struggle, throwing us into a tailspin. It's not surprising that this happens, as we're constantly challenged by TUNA (*and I don't mean a big fish for those that suffer from ichthyophobia*) – Turbulent, Uncertain, Novel and Ambiguous - situations as we go about our personal and working lives. Sometimes this creates 'stress' and sometimes 'stress' comes as part of our decision-making process. A wealth of research concludes that stress (*a complex phenomenon*) is a significant element in the quality of our decision-making. This chapter is focused on the inherent stresses (*time pressures, information overload, decision complexity and uncertainty*) in work and life, how they impact, and how you can overcome stress to improve the quality of your decisions.

I've seen many different decision-making processes play out in different environments faced. As part of my role, I look to support the decision-making of senior decision-makers so that when faced with a significant challenge, they don't become 'stuck,' (analysis paralysis - *a situation in which an individual or group is unable to move forward with a decision as a result of overanalysing data or overthinking a problem*) and can move forward with key decisions in a timely and confident manner. I am not always successful in achieving this as stress impacts people differently.

When working with a Senior Management Team, the phone system was switched off, to add another dimension of stress to the participants during a desktop exercise. This added to the complexity (*How will we communicate?*) and uncertainty (*What else can go wrong?*) of the situation. This distortion on the situation impacted on one team member's ability to process information to hand, which was now perceived as conflicting (we had kept communications open via walkie-talkies) in that we could communicate, but it was limited. There was also the issue that people were not comfortable using a walkie-talkie (Press – Pause - Speak). As a team, I had the utmost confidence that this team would work through these stressors and perform well. However, it became very apparent early on that this team member could not get past the telephony issue and was stuck. It became clear that the now-stressed decision-maker was displaying riskier behaviours, ignoring or misinterpreting critical information, and discrediting evidence that did not fit with their personal decision-making process. The team dynamic, usually strong, was significantly impacted during the exercise.

This person was a highly capable individual, with a proven track record, and made decisions daily on complex issues. It was however clear this day, and it was certainly an off-day on their behalf, that the additional stressors, impacted that individual's decision-making capability. As research shows, stress can negatively impact a decision-maker's ability to process data and information, create fear and/or indecisiveness, interfere with balanced decision-making, alter the decision maker's critical thinking, and lead to delays in action, even when doing so results in a poor decision outcome.

2. STRESSORS

The stressors identified earlier in this chapter – *time pressures, information overload, decision complexity and uncertainty* are described below. These stressors do not work in isolation. As one stress manifests itself, there are often other stressors at play, as will be seen below. Over time these stressors can significantly impact on a decision-maker.

A. TIME PRESSURES

Time is a crucial resource. It impacts as tensions build when faced with time limits in the decision-making process, meaning time pressures are triggered, impacting not only on the decision-maker's behaviour but also their decision-making. When faced with TUNA environments, quality decisions require more cognitive ability to process available information and, ideally, less distraction of time pressures. Earlier in the chapter, the decision-maker was already in a situation that would simulate a stressful situation and, subsequently, added time pressures to their decision-making. The added complexity, due to the telephony issue, ensured that these time pressures became more sharpened in that individual's mind. This led to the individual basing their decision-making on the time pressures faced rather than walking through their normal decision-making process.

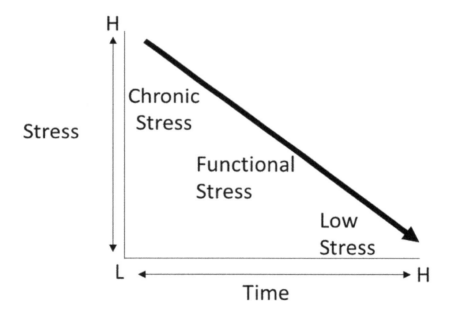

Figure 01: Time Pressure (Author's own)

B. INFORMATION OVERLOAD

Current research suggests that 'information overload' is recognised as having an adverse effect on decision-making. However, as we encounter complex environments, we are faced with more and more decisions. This leads to decision fatigue (something we will look at shortly), and with the volume of information available (and increasing!) to decision-makers who are always connected to endless sources of information, produces too much information to be processed effectively. As indicated in the diagram below, in situations of time pressure, the quality of decision-making increases with information load but then decreases as decision-makers get caught in the trap of information overload, and the quality of decision-making reduces. If, in a perfect state, there were no time pressures when faced with decision-making, the impact of information overload is significantly reduced. However, in reality, there will always be time pressures at play.

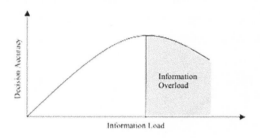

Figure 02: Information Overload

C. DECISION COMPLEXITY

As we find ourselves challenged by TUNA environments, there are time pressures, significantly more information available than we want (or need), and countless options that we either simplify (to our detriment in some cases), or we believe we will make the right decision based on our experience and knowledge (Confidence Bias). As Schon (1983) articulated in his research, a decision-maker *'must make sense of an uncertain situation that initially makes no sense.'* The challenge is the situation will likely be *'unique, dynamic, unprecedented, difficult to define or bound, and have no clear set of solutions.'* Where the situation has many dynamic components and interactions, and is not fully understood, it provides a significant hurdle for decision-makers as they try to understand the dynamic range at play. As Keith Grint explained in his research on 'Wicked Problems,' we're aware of a problem but it is not clear exactly what the problem actually is. This makes decision-making unpredictable.

D. UNCERTAINTY

The impact of uncertainty on decision-making has received considerable research focus over the years. The inability to eliminate or reduce uncertainty from decision-making considerably inhibits the effectiveness of decision-making and requires the adoption of methods that help to reduce, or to manage uncertainty.

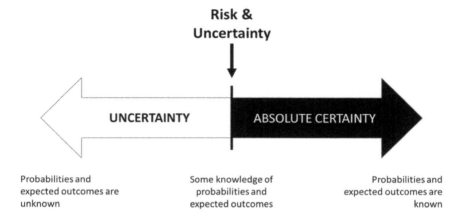

Figure 03: Decision-Making under Uncertainty

Research shows that unfamiliar situations, hindered by complexity and cognitive overload, have a significant impact on decision-making. In other words, when uncertainty is a component of the decision-making process, there is a tendency to be drawn to what seems to be a more certain outcome. Risk aversion is another problem that surfaces when dealing with uncertainty. Decision-making is influenced by the mindset to risk. An individual who is risk averse will focus on possible negative outcomes from options available. An individual with a risk tolerant mindset will no doubt see the potential positive options from the decision to be made.

In my case, as the stressors started to spiral out of my control, I lost trust in my ability to make the right decision, especially in my career. This had a detrimental impact on my career path, and even in situations that I would normally have been confident in, I started to second-guess myself. This began to have a damaging effect on my physical and mental wellbeing. In an effort to rectify the situation, I over-extended myself to try and break the 'bad streak' I felt I was on. This led to trying to function as normal, not show signs of weakness to others, and put in more and more effort to pull back and get back on an even keel.

3. DECISION FATIGUE

Another factor to consider is the impact on decision-making from decision fatigue. Decision fatigue can be defined as *'when the mind becomes fatigued after a sustained period of decision making. Making decisions is a cognitively taxing process, and decision-making ability declines after long sequences of decisions'*. Essentially if the decision-maker has been challenged to make decision after decision, over a certain period of time, the quality of decisions starts to break down as their cognitive capabilities fall short due to 'ego depletion'. As 'ego depletion' impacts, decision-makers start to make compromises in their decision-making by looking for the path of least resistance cognitively, leading to poor decision choices, and in some instances, end up making no decision at all.

4. VALUES BASED DECISION-MAKING

In recent times, after making some poor decisions, and starting to question my own judgement on life and career decisions, I revised my decision-making approach. Admittedly there are still some decisions that are out of my control that have to be made, but for the decisions I do have control over, I have moved to a values-based decision-making (VBDM) model to support my decision-making process.

When your values and purposes are aligned, it becomes apparent that decision-making becomes less stressful, as we better understand what shapes our critical thinking and are less confused and erratic in our decision-making. Benjamin Franklin summed it up nicely when he said, *'We stand at the crossroads, each minute, each hour, each day, making choices. We choose the thoughts we allow ourselves to think, the passions we allow ourselves to feel, and the actions we allow ourselves to perform. Each choice is made in the context of whatever value systems we have selected to govern our lives. In selecting that value system, we are in a very real way, making the most important choice we will ever make.'*

Values are a fundamental part of behaviour, especially, in the decision-making process because they shape the basis of an individual's perspective. When options are benchmarked against values, the right decision quickly becomes evident. Aligning values to decisions additionally ensures critical thinking about the outcomes of those decisions.

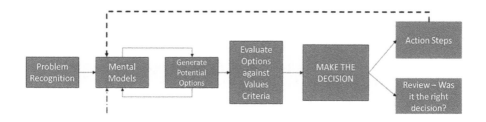

Figure 04: Value Based Decision-Making Model (Author's own)

4. OVERCOMING STRESS

So how do we overcome stress and the impacts on, or from, decision-making? People will have their own 'hacks' for dealing with stress. Some of the approaches I take are documented below (and I hope they help in some way):

A. 'CONDOR' MOMENT

Often when faced with a decision, and concerned about the time pressures and complexity involved, it can help to take a 'Condor' moment. For those too young to remember the TV adverts, I highly recommend you view the advert on YouTube! In a nutshell, a 'Condor' moment is taking a step back, seeing the bigger picture and taking time to consider the next decision. Although we talked about time pressures earlier on in this chapter, these pressures are often of our own thinking so taking time to have a 'Condor' moment should not have a negative impact on that decision.

B. USE OF CHECKLISTS

Some people love them, and some people loathe them. Over time, I have come to rely on checklists to focus my energies on the important decisions I face, either in my career or life. In this context, it helps to lessen my cognitive juggling by having a list of decisions that have to be made that day. I am able to whittle down the options available to me by applying the values criteria I benchmark decisions against. It gives me something tangible to show others and discuss the options available or receive feedback that opens up other possibilities I had not considered. Most importantly it allows me to prioritise important decisions to be made. I can then give the important decisions the vitality that is needed to work through the complexity and uncertainty (and get some quick wins under the belt), if under time pressures.

C. INFORMED INTUITION

Use your gut. Not the 'lucky guess' intuition though, but informed intuition. 'Informed intuition' is developed over a period of time and is largely shaped by your past experiences and knowledge. 'Informed intuition' is differentiated from 'intuition' by the decision-maker seeking more solid proof from which to validate their initial intuitive options. It can avoid many of the perils of intuitive decision-making as it combines further rational evaluation of additional data that might be available. This combination of intuition (experience, knowledge) and added analysis generates well-rounded decisions by approaching decisions through a different lens. It boosts the decrease in the probability of poor decision-making and is gradually becoming an adopted approach to decision-making in today's TUNA environments.

D. VITALITY

The most important aspect for me, sitting alongside my values, is vitality. It means different things to different people, but for me, it is having that balance of physical, mental and emotional strength. I can pinpoint when I started to make bad decisions, to a point in time that I suffered significant leg injuries that have caused lifelong complications that impacted my physical and mental wellbeing and proceeded to throw my well-balanced vitality out of kilter. Over time this pushed my values and purpose out of alignment. It took a significant period of time, and help from others, to find my vitality again. As that vitality has been strengthening and strengthening, I aligned my values and purpose again and those poor decisions started to evaporate. It has taken time to rectify the damage caused by my poor decision-making, but I am now in a position where I can trust myself and move forward again.

ABOUT THE AUTHOR

Colm is an outlier amongst this book's cohort of authors. He did not have a phenomenally successful military career, or create multi-million income generating companies. Nor has he held any senior roles where he has been an influencer or a driver of success. So (*and he himself has asked this question too*) how has he managed to get involved with such a successful cohort of people?

Colm provides realistic and directional leadership to support and improve decision-making by Senior Management Teams when faced with turbulent, uncertain, complex and ambiguous situations. He provides an evidence-based, yet innovative, approach to help drive continuous improvement in organisations' resilience capabilities. He is an insightful and curious individual who is a great listener and focuses on getting to the crux of issues, applying his knowledge and practical experience to help shape potential issues. He is a strong advocate for mentoring and coaching, especially for younger or junior members of his teams, to assist them to learn from their mistakes and build their confidence to push forward in their careers.

He is still passionate and always learning.

Outside the work environment, he is an ardent Liverpool fan, and has managed to turn his wife and young son into fellow supporters. A big advocate of the outdoors, and despite some limitations, he still loves a good bimble in the countryside. He is even mulling over a PhD …

Now, more than ever, there is a need for physical and mental wellbeing. It provides a bedrock for long term sustainable living, allowing us to operate at our optimum.

4

JAMIE WATKINS

'MIND AND BODY' - MAKING THE CONNECTION

INTRODUCTION

Now, more than ever, there is a need for physical and mental wellbeing. It provides a bedrock for long term sustainable living, allowing us to operate at our optimum. Especially with all 7.5 billion of us human beings (note the term 'human beings' not 'human doings') living through a pandemic.

Self-awareness is the start of the waking up process. So many of us live our lives on auto-pilot. Day by day. Week by week. Year by year. Like zombies. Body and mind disconnected.

My name is Jamie Watkins and at 39 years old I received my wake-up call. At that time in my life, I had already setup, built, and sold my first three businesses; but I'd also pushed my mind and body to breaking point.

Now, at 45, I feel more alive than ever. I've awakened to what is important. I've learnt to let go, trusting and loving the process. 'The Journey is the Destination.' I have three beautiful children and a wonderful wife of 25 years. I now have balance, living life the middle way.

I am thankful day by day for so many great people around me who enrich my life.

In this chapter I will give you insights into my journey so far. I'll look at business but also at life, growth, pain, purpose, hope, love, joy and positivity. I hope you can take something from it to help you in the same way it's helped me. This is by no means the last chapter of my book as I've still got so much to learn… but for now, it's an insight into my world where living a happy and healthy life is achievable when you understand that when you 'get your mind right, you get your life right.'

THE MILLIONAIRE DETERMINATION

From a young age, I was looking to earn my own money and make my way in the world. I had the standard 'paper rounds' but with a strong entrepreneurial spirit, found ways to hustle; I had a successful enterprise making, buying and selling computer games at school. I also had a determined will to win; excelling at snooker having a 93 break at 13 years of age and playing (never beating) the now three time world-champion Mark Williams. Alongside my love of house music, partying hard and playing football on Saturday and Sunday every week meant I left school with five GCSEs and ended up working at McDonald's. As I look back this taught me customer service and teamwork at a young age. I enjoyed my time there.

At 19, and working in various factory jobs, something changed. I had a clear feeling that it was time to improve my life. How could I provide for a family I thought? I had already gained a grounding in electrics from my dad. It felt an obvious choice to try and get an electrical apprenticeship. I got lucky. Yuasa accepted. Six years later after working at Yuasa Batteries Europe training as an engineer and studying part-time at university, I gained an ONC, HNC, HND and a Degree. I am thankful for so many people that helped mentor me, there we so many. One worth a special mention: Ieuan Davies. Took him out every Christmas for lunch, loved him. He passed last year. Thank you Leuan RIP; you taught me so much 'show up & work hard.' After this in 1998, I left Yuasa to go on to complete a full-time master's in computer studies where in parallel I set up my first business whilst starting work as a part-time lecturer too.

The next 20 years were busy. Very busy. I was determined to be a millionaire. Nothing would stop me. Some weeks I worked 80-100 hours while at RUMM, an online energy management business which we started in 2002 at University. It consumed me. Did it all, from making the tea, to selling complex million-pound deals to multinational blue chips when we had just '50p in the bank.' I travelled the UK and Europe to see customers and set up an 'office' in the USA. Develop the team, secure investment, look after our customers and build the business were my mantras. It was a rollercoaster. I worked hard. Played hard. I kept physically fit, but at no time did I consider the health of my mind.

Our Investor and Chairman at the time, Eric Lewis OBE, kept shouting at me to slow down. I did not understand it then. Now I do. He had the wisdom. Thank you, Eric. RIP.

After 20 years of hard graft, and with thanks to an incredible team around me, we achieved a major goal. I could not have done it without the support of my wife Fran. She's been by my side through all the ups and downs. And so, on April 1st 2015 after a long and tiring two-year process, which included many trips back and forth to London with my good friend and Co Founder Dr Steve Lloyd, we sold 'our baby' RUMM to Npower, turning the heads of all the major energy companies. It made front page of the Financial Times. One of the biggest deals in Europe, the business sold for 47 times profit. Yes 47.

The blood sweat and tears seemed worth it. It felt good. I felt good.

But it only lasted a short time.

2015. 39 years old. I'd set up, built and sold three businesses: but for what? It gave my family financial freedom, which I will always be deeply thankful for, but it was not without sacrifice. There were only 24 hours in a day, but I lived as if they could be lived without any need to recharge myself.

ROCK BOTTOM

In 2014, in the midst of my million-miles-an-hour lifestyle, I had no idea that my mind and body were in total discord. I ended up learning the hard way.

Physically I was at my fittest. Ten days before running the London Marathon I was in the best shape of my life. I'd run the Cardiff Half Marathon in 1 hour 22 minutes the year before. I'd raced lots of Spartans over the UK with Andrew, my PT, finishing high up on the leaderboards. I felt great. I felt strong. Nothing could touch me, or so I thought.

Ten days before London I accepted a 'plank challenge.' Ego got the better of me. Down on the mat I went. Never going to quit. 1,2,3….6,8… Held for 10 minutes. Won the competition. Ego happy. Went to work at 7am after a cold shower and protein shake. I took on my day at RUMM with the team. It was a great day, one of joy and feeling good about myself.

The next day. Saturday 6am. I woke up. In pain. My back had gone. I was unable to walk and spent the weekend in bed, in tears. All the training; 60-80 miles per week. For what? A stupid egoic moment. I was in serious pain, my back was in spasms and my mind was drowning in the thoughts of 'how could I run 26.2 miles in 10 days?'

Race day in London arrived. 25 of my family and friends were there. I was aiming to raise £5k for my best friend who had nearly died from a rare blood cancer. The pressure was on. I felt the nerves deep in my stomach. I tightened my back brace, swallowed some extra strength pain killers and the gun went off. Pain. Seeing my three children with my family and friends gave me the lift I needed at 10km. It hurt, but I would not stop. My focus was 13 miles. Got there in 1.33, I was half-way. Keep going, my mantra. At 20 miles I hit the wall. More pain killers. I finished the race in 3.26 but it hurt, really hurt.

Two weeks later a trip to Bupa led to diagnosis of Pars defect, a crack in the spine. What do I do? Stop running? My head was in a spin. I felt broken. I asked the consultant, 'Do I stop running?' He said 'if you love it then, no, get your body strong again.' 'How,' I asked? His answer, 'Yoga. Get your core strong. Not your abs. Put some scaffolding up to protect your body. Day by day rebuild.'

Little did I know that this simple instruction would change my life. It was a blessing. Yoga was my entry point into meditation. My path was being established. My yoga teacher helped me hugely 1-2-1. She saw that I loved the breath. I felt it. The mind and body connection. There it was.

After a few months, she connected me to a Meditation teacher to deepen my practice. It became my purpose to get fit again, this time not just physically but also mentally. And not just to run. More importantly, to serve others with this new profound understanding of the mind and body connection via the breath.

The road was long. Bumpy. It was a tough, dark period. Day by day, all I could do was to show up for myself.

My mother rang in my head, 'what your mind believes your body achieves.' Had to get a routine. Get up early. Eat well. Re-build. It was a dark place. But out of darkness comes light. The light shone again. Brightly.

Whilst we all seek external gratification to make us happy, my journey into yoga, meditation and mindfulness meant I woke up to the fact that happiness is within. As human beings, we all want to be happy. It's in our human nature. We have a choice. All too often we search for it outside of ourselves. We seek to amass 'things' that only serve to make our life cluttered. When we seek external gratification rather than looking within, it causes us physical and mental stress.

It turns out that happiness is already there, right inside us all. It always has been.

After two years, many hours, weeks and months of yoga, meditation, eating well, reduced alcohol and more exercise, I felt more focused than ever. So, when my teacher said the words, 'you should meet Gelong Thubten,' I felt that this meant something more.

On Thursday 26th September 2016 in Cardiff, Thubten and I had a chance meeting. Within five minutes we connected. It was real. I told him we would change the world. Thubten smiled. 'You are the SAS of the mind,' I said. 'I can hopefully build the business side of things. Let's make it happen.'

THE BIRTH OF SAMTEN

Two weeks later, I found myself on a seven-hour car drive to Scotland. It was my calling. Spending the weekend in the monastery with Thubten was meant to be. We chatted. Meditated. Walked. It felt right. Samten was born.

Samten, the Tibetan word 'to meditate,' is a joint venture. Gelong Thubten is a world-renowned Buddhist monk and New York Times best seller. Samten, in its first stages, is a meditation and mindfulness app, but it will become much more.

Thubten and I share a similar story of spiritual awakening. We understand our purpose is to serve, to give back and help others free themselves from their monkey mind. We all have a monkey mind. It's what gives you between 60 to 80,000 thoughts every day. But, believing them all only brings trouble as the monkey is innately negative, always ruminating and worrying. Being able to stand back and observe them with clarity is profound and brings mind and body into connection.

Our aim for the business is to give 50% of our profits to charity. It's been a very challenging project, but we have stayed true to our purpose and intention. To help others. With meditation and mindfulness now in my world, I can deal with the fact that we have fallen down many times, but I know we will never give up. www.samten.co

Our New App is coming out in quarter two this year, watch this space… I'm personally very thankful for John Jepson and Simon Delve who have believed in our purpose. The future is bright at Samten.

MUSIC – 'IT'S ALWAYS BEEN ABOUT THE MUSIC'

Whilst I may have changed many things since my youth, the one constant that has remained is house music. It's in my DNA and absolutely one of my 'whys'.

With my fast-paced life, there was little room for music for a while, but in 2013 we connected with DJ, Glen Horsborough, and his podcast, 'Let There Be House.' Fast forward to 2021, we have an established brand now with over 200,000 followers and zero employees. A community and movement of house heads that has become family.

In 2016, I reached out to Simon Dunmore of Defected Records, one of the biggest, and arguably the best, house labels in the world. Our energies connected. A few months after we met, I ran a strategy session in Ibiza. Was asked to join the board as Chief Strategy Officer. Love and respect to the team that has now developed a 7.5 million strong community, hold 200+ parties across the world each year and ship quality merchandise globally. It is a beautiful business.

The final link in the music chain happened in the summer of 2019, when I was asked to invest into a music festival in Wales; 'Escape.' This turned into an acquisition, along with three other festivals. The timing could not have been worse, as no-one is immune to a world pandemic. But we will keep the faith, hold the vision and trust the process until we can party together again.

Music | BSE (www.blueskyequity.co.uk/music)

STAYING TRUE TO THE PATH

From a boy who grew up loving football, snooker, and house music, to the father, husband, friend and businessman I am today, I now truly appreciate the value in looking after your body and your mind.

Without them both being in great shape, how can you operate over the long term for:

- Yourself
- Your family & friends
- Your teams

The link between body and mind is unbreakable. Physical and mental health leads to emotional resilience. We all need it for life and business. A great Zen quote is 'the only thing that's permanent is impermanence.'

But life can often prove distracting. So how do I stay true to my path?

ROUTINE

I find it key to get up early and establish a good routine each day that feeds both body and mind. I listen to lots of podcasts and gain insights from some very well-respected individuals, Jay Shetty (On Purpose), Simon Sinek, Lewis Howes (Podcast 1073 is special on positive thinking & the science of mind), Tim Ferriss, Dave Aspery, and Tony Robbins to name a few.

MEDITATION

Each morning and evening I meditate and focus on three things that I'm grateful for. Just to be is enough. Be grateful for the little things – always.

FOOD & DRINK

I drink good drinks early – ginger, lemon and honey. I won't drink coffee until later and then it's a Bullet Proof coffee – I recommend you try them out.

When it comes to food, don't use the word diet – it's not sustainable. Instead, I use a framework of intermittent fasting and eat foods that are good for my gut. (See https://www.getferal.co.uk/ and https://thefastingmethod. com/ for more detailed information.)

Reduce or cut out alcohol completely.

I'm also a big believer in the benefits of CBD and am currently working with a company to launch a new brand into the market. Cannibinoids found in the hemp plant, are known to positively affect our digestive and nervous systems, joints, muscles and skin. Find out more at www.awakeearth.co.uk

Also supplement with vitamins to suit your needs and ensure you get a regular health check as you see fit.

MOVE

Walk, run, jog, do yoga, swim, cycle. Just move in whatever way you can or want to. It's key to producing the endorphins that keep our mind smiling. Make sure you warm up and cool down. I also integrate Wim Hoff breathing and cold exposure techniques. For me, the benefits are undeniable, both in the immediate and long term. See www.wimhofmethod.com for more details.

STAY CONNECTED

Human connection. We all need it. Think about what you are doing. Use email as just that. Email. It's a replacement for mail that used to take days to arrive. Don't feel you have to respond straight way. Or at all. Now we have people texting saying 'I've sent you an email,' but it's all wrong. Learn to stand back. Turn off your notifications. Turn off your phone. Be in control of your phone, not the other way around. Use airplane mode at night. This has helped me run my world. I have eight email accounts to operate, but more importantly I have three children and a beautiful wife. We need our quality time too.

GIVE BACK

I've now raised over £150,000 for various charities and am an ambassador for Cancer Research Wales. We have lost too many close family and friends to this disease. 1 in 2 people will get cancer and we need to find new ways to deal with it. This is my purpose too. My respect goes to Dale Evans at CRW who tirelessly finds ways to generate funding.

SLEEP MORE

I have learnt during the past 12 months, just how important sleep is. I've discovered that sleep is the 'cornerstone' to good health, and everything we do. In the past, I was disrespectful towards my sleep habits. I'd work 60-80 hours per week and boast about sleeping only 5-6 hours per night. In the following chapter, Tammy McPherson demonstrates the science behind how lack of sleep is detrimental to our health.

This year I have created a routine before bed, including meditation, and am now grateful to be sleeping 8 hours per night. Since purchasing an Oura ring (activity tracker), I have been able to track my sleep not stress levels, and this has proven to be transformational. If you make one purchase in 2021, I recommend this. As the Dala Lama once said, 'The best form of meditation is sleep.'

USE KPIS IN BUSINESS AND IN LIFE

Measurement is key, don't underestimate this. Use the tools and tech that are around you, but stay in control of them. Set your goals. Share your vision with teams and family. Keep it simple and easily updatable. As Lord Kelvin said, 'If you can not measure it, you can not improve it.'

And in doing all these, you'll have the benefit of boosting your immunity for now and the future. I'm a big fan of Greg Whyte, so please check out his website Greg Whyte - Physical Activity Expert for more details.

STAY TRUE

To charter the rocky road of the pandemic in 2020 I've lived and breathed all of the things I talk about to keep my mind and body connected, and I feel in the best shape of my life. In November 2020 I did a half marathon every day. A combination of running and walking, finishing the month on 750km to raise money for MIND and build some awareness across my social media channels.

I was always racing from one thing to another. I still race sometimes. That's how it is in business and life, but now I have balance. I see it and feel it. I am blessed to have beautiful family and friends around me that enrich my life. In parallel, my business world does not feel like a job anymore as I'm now living out my 'whys'. I get it. All of it.

'Trust and love the process,' is now my mantra. Embodying all I do day by day. Never compromising my values; open, honest, trustworthy, transparent, and operate at all times with integrity. This is me, now and forever. I've also made the decision to not consume alcohol for a year. In August 2021 I will reach this goal. If the clarity remains as strong as it does now, I may never drink again.

My path is clear; Music, Meditation and giving back. Helping others. My why. What is yours? It's ok if you don't know it yet, you will at the right time. For me to live out my 'why' I need to stay 'fit.' Not just physically.

My new mantra; 'Passion with a Purpose'

I am deeply grateful now, and meditate on it daily. I now have the tools to keep my body and mind in great shape. I am thankful for some great teachers along my path. There have been many, including my three beautiful children who keep it real, day by day. I also want to give thanks to my mother and father who were so supportive in those early years and throughout my life. Don't take life so seriously. I'm learning.

Meditation has given me a deep appreciation for what matters. Gratitude is at the core, partnered with love and kindness. Focus and concentrate. Understand the middle way. Develop wisdom. Know that we are not our monkey mind. We are the observer, the one who is always free.

ABOUT THE AUTHOR

A passionate serial entrepreneur having setup, built & sold his first three businesses by age 39 in the engineering, software, and energy markets. Now setup and investing in seven more via Blue Sky Equity; a private company he founded in early 2017.

'It starts with why...people don't buy what you do they buy why you do it.'

Find and know your why, when you do you will never work another day in your life.

His why;
Giving back
Music & Meditation
Sharing hope, love, and positivity

Your business is not what solely defines you. It is what you do day to day that does. Fall down lots but never give up. Developed and continue to develop a growth mindset. Enjoying a new world now with much more balance & clarity. Relish a challenge. Humble & Honest. Love family & friends.

'You can't connect the dots looking forward only back.' A great Steve Jobs quote.

His Mantras
'Get your mind right. Get your life right'
'Be consistent at being consistent'
'The Journey is the Destination'
'Trust and love the process'
'Every day's a school day'
'Purpose with Passion'
'Show up'

Having fun working with varying businesses and organisations across a range of sectors now; Music. Meditation. Wellness. Property. CBD. Technology. Charity.

Jamie led the sale of RUMM to Npower (RWE) which concluded on

April 1st 2015. One of the largest energy deals in Europe. He won many company awards whilst at the helm of RUMM; top entrepreneur in Wales 2007 & inclusion in the Who's Who of Britain's Business Elite - less than 2% of directors under 40 achieve this.

A process control engineer that studied six years part time whilst working in industry to get a degree. Then did a full time Masters in Computers, where he went onto setup his first business.

Strategically, Commercially, Technically & Operationally strong. Sales & Marketing for over two decades. A focused individual who is driven to achieve the task in hand. Knows & understands what needs to get done & gets its done.

His love of house music has seen some exciting collaborations. With Glen Horsborough from Let There Be House in 2014. Working closely with Simon Dunmore of Defected Records alongside Wez Saunders since 2017. His third collaboration is with festivals in Wales since late 2019; poor timing with a global pandemic but embodying his Mantra 'trust & love the process'

He has setup and invested into a property business; Frrind Developments with a long time good friend, and recently invested into a new CBD brand; Awake Earth.

He has also developed the meditation and mindfulness app 'Samten' with world-renowned Buddhist Monk and New York Times Bestseller, Gelong Thubten. The aim for Samten, is to give back 50% of profits to charity.

He sits on the board of Cranfield University's Masters in Strategic Marketing and is also an Ambassador for Cancer Research Wales.

His determination has also seen him excel in other areas of his life. As a young man, he was playing snooker to high standards, even playing alongside (future) world champions with a 97 break at 13. He loved his football playing every Saturday & Sunday. Physical fitness was always important. He is going to pick up a cue again post pandemic…

Jamie has competed in numerous Marathons and Spartans across the UK. Raising over £150k for Cancer Research after breaking a world record and trekking across Iceland in 2019. In November 2020 he completed a challenge for charity, running/walking a half-marathon every day throughout the month, getting to 750km and raising money for MIND.

He now mediates daily and embodies a much more mindful way of living with his family. Knowing when to put his phone onto airplane mode to 'Just Be' & paying respect to sleep. Living in Wales with his wife of 25 years, and three beautiful children his life is now more balanced. Family & friends are close to his heart. Hope, love, and positivity are what he embodies.

'Work smart. Stay humble. Be kind. Show up. Never give up on your dreams. Never.'

Since the creation of Edison's lightbulb, our sleep patterns have changed significantly. A few hundred years ago we would sleep after dark and wake with the dawn. With our ever-changing, ever-busy modern lives, sleep in many cultures is now undervalued.

TAMMY MCPHERSON
5 WHY YOU SHOULDN'T LOSE SLEEP OVER YOUR HEALTH

Thomas Edison said, *'Sleep is a criminal waste of time.*

I have always had a complicated relationship with sleep. I vacillate between feeling enjoyment, frustration at not being able to sleep when I need to, and guilt if I sleep too much. Growing up in a hard-working Australian family, sleep was considered an indulgence rather than an important biological process. In my family household, anyone who slept eight hours or longer was awarded the sobriquet of 'sleepy head.' That manifested as a constant desire to sleep less so I could achieve more.

Since the creation of Edison's lightbulb, our sleep patterns have changed significantly. A few hundred years ago we would sleep after dark and wake with the dawn. With our ever-changing, ever-busy modern lives, sleep in many cultures is now undervalued.

With conflicting media stories and prominent leaders telling us they sleep as little as four hours per night, and many people consistently staying awake until the early hours of the morning, I wonder if we are in the midst of a global sleep crisis. I wanted to get under the metaphorical covers and find out.

Thankfully sleep has fascinated humanity over the ages and equipped me with an abundance of research papers and literature ideal for my quest to understand our current sleep status. I poured through large-scale epidemiological studies and spoke to a number of sleep experts to understand the science behind sleep and the insights are staggering.

We spend up to a third of our lives sleeping. It's essential for good health and general wellbeing. Sleep helps cleanse the brain of toxins and is known to boost our immune system and cardiovascular health. Research has shown enough of a connection between insufficient sleep and cancer that the World Health Organisation now classifies any form of shift work as a 'probable carcinogen' due to the interference of sleep-wake rhythms.

How well we rest plays a huge role in our professional life. With adequate sleep, our brains are better able to link information in abstract ways that support effective problem solving and creative thought. Our decision-making abilities are enhanced, as is our capacity to stay objective, patient and calm. I'm sure the idiom 'got out of the wrong side of bed' has applied to more than just me on occasion!

At a deeper level, the neuroscience behind sleep can show us just how much it can affect both our work and personal lives.

WHAT ACTUALLY HAPPENS WHEN WE FALL ASLEEP?

During the day, the electrochemical activity in our brain generates byproducts called sleep factors. These sleep factors promote sleep and each have a different role to play. Adenosine is one such byproduct of metabolic and electrical activity in your neurons. During the day adenosine builds up and promotes sleep by influencing various biological pathways that affect our sleep-wake state. It gives us that 'sleepy feeling' we're all familiar with.

Our sleep cycles go through four stages of non-rapid eye movement (NREM) sleep, followed by a stage of rapid eye movement (REM) sleep. Both have important and different roles to play. We experience a new sleep cycle approximately every 90 to 110 minutes and the proportion of REM and NREM sleep changes with each cycle.

NREM sleep is classified in stages 1 to 4, with 1 and 2 being light sleep, and stages 3 and 4 being deep sleep. Bear with me, this becomes important as we discuss what happens at each stage of sleep. When falling asleep, (NREM 1 and 2), we experience a decrease in our heart rate and temperature, and our neural activity begins to slow. Moving into deep sleep (NREM 3 and 4), the body and brain begin to rejuvenate, and our immune system receives a boost. During this stage we consolidate our memories and move them to our brain's 'long term storage.' It is considered difficult to be woken from stage 4 NREM, with no eye activity or muscle movement experienced during this time. If woken from this deep sleep, you are likely to feel groggy and disoriented. Sleep scientists call this sleep inertia.

Transitioning into REM, our brain wave activity starts to speed up again, and we can experience dreams, sometimes strange and nonsensical, sometimes not. During REM sleep we piece together information and data our brain has stored during the day, and in some cases, can find solutions to previously difficult problems. It is widely believed this state of sleep can foster creativity and through history there are examples of dreams used as inspiration. Indeed, one such apocryphal story is that Mary Shelley based the story of Frankenstein on a dream she had. She claims the idea 'arose before my mind with a vividness far beyond the usual bounds of reverie'.

'My dreams were all my own; I accounted for them to nobody; they were my refuge when annoyed - my dearest pleasure when free.' ~ Mary Shelley

Throughout the night, our brain constantly competes for NREM and REM sleep. The proportion of NREM and REM sleep changes with each cycle as the night goes on. Early in the night, deep NREM sleep is greater, but as we move into the second half of the night, the cycles are dominated by REM and light NREM sleep. So, the implications of waking prematurely, or sleeping less, are that you could miss out on much-needed REM sleep.

Our brain is cleansed

During my fact-finding mission, I was intrigued to learn that only very recently scientists discovered a cleansing system in our brain which is active during sleep but largely disengaged during wakefulness. We knew it existed within the body, (our lymphatic system), but it has only recently come to light that the brain has its own cleansing process, using a unique system of vascular tunnels to eliminate toxic proteins. Maiken Nedergaard, a Danish neuroscientist who led the discovery, coined this the glymphatic system since it is similar to the lymphatic system but involves brain cells known as glial cells. This system works at different speeds during sleep with deep NREM sleep providing the best conditions for the neuroprotective benefits of sleep. When we are in sleep deprivation, the glymphatic system does not have the time needed to perform its role and toxins can build up leading to cognitive, behavioural and judgement challenges. This waste processing is imperative in supporting learning and memory but goes further by regulating our moods and even impacting our sexual appetite.

Our memory is enhanced

Neuroscientists hypothesise that sleep contributes to the processes of memory and brain plasticity. Over the past decade, there has been a substantial body of evidence to support sleep dependent memory processing. Long-term episodic memory that is acquired while we are awake throughout the day is initially stored in the hippocampus region in the brain. Episodic memory involves specific events and situations you have experienced such as your first kiss or the gifts you received on your last birthday. During deep NREM sleep, these memories are transferred to the cortex where data is stored for recollection over a longer period. The brain further cements the memory by replaying the information, which strengthens and reinforces the corresponding synapses for long-term storage.

WHAT ABOUT SLEEP (OR LACK OF IT) AND OUR HEALTH?

We all know that eating well and exercising regularly is key to a healthy lifestyle. Intuitively, we also know that sleep is equally important, and is needed to rejuvenate us. A lack of sleep can take a toll on our health, and our bodies will usually give us some obvious signs when we've had too little or even too much sleep.

It is common for individuals with mental wellness challenges to have chronic sleep issues; cardiovascular disease, cancers and chronic inflammation have also been linked to a lack of quality sleep.

Through large-scale epidemiological studies, we know that adults need between 7 to 9 hours of sleep per night. Once we drop below this, mortality and morbidity rates increase. What is interesting is that sleep quality, independent of sleep quantity, is associated with health risks. Good-quality sleep ensures we have both NREM and REM sleep. Simply going back to sleep to 'catch up' after a restless night won't necessarily provide you with the benefits of a good-quality sleep. Sleeping less leads to sleep debt, which can build over time. Sleeping longer hours over the weekend unfortunately does not make up for mid-week sleep deprivation. The best way to overcome sleep debt is to slowly build up more sleep time over the long term.

Lack of sleep, and accumulation of sleep debt, is linked to immune deficiency. A recent study of healthy adults showed a significant number of genes are distorted with just two hours less sleep. Meanwhile, four hours of sleep deprivation in one night has been linked to a 70% decrease in the activity of natural killer cells, which play a vital role in eliminating dangerous and unwanted elements in the body. Another interesting study has shown that if you are sleep deprived a week before receiving the flu vaccine, your body will produce 50% less antibody response than average. Sleeping seven hours or less is linked to an increase in the likelihood of contracting rhinovirus, one of the viruses that cause the common cold.

Not only is the immune system compromised but sleep disorders, such as sleep apnoea, affect the respiratory system and exacerbate existing conditions. Within the digestive system, lack of sleep is believed to reduce leptin levels and raise ghrelin, which can stimulate the appetite as well as lowering the body's tolerance for glucose, affecting insulin resistance.

Poor sleep quality may also be a factor in the development of Alzheimer's disease. It was recently discovered that the glymphatic system helps clear away beta-amyloid, a sticky and toxic protein that has been connected to Alzheimer's. A recent study found that individuals with lower quality sleep are more likely to have beta-amyloid accumulation in the brain years later. Alzheimer's is also associated with sleep disorders, such as insomnia and sleep apnoea, which further facilitates the build up of beta-amyloid. The connection between sleep deprivation and Alzheimer's remains a field of significant active research.

HOW DOES DISRUPTED SLEEP MANIFEST ITSELF?

When we are sleep deprived we forget simple things. The hippocampus is an area in the brain that aids memory and learning, and sleep debt can disrupt normal functioning. After a bad night of sleep you might find that you can't recall the word you are looking for, can't remember a name, or retain numbers like you usually do.

There is emerging evidence that REM sleep supports a process of affective brain homeostasis (balance), which is helpful for social and emotional functioning and decision-making. The amygdala, known as the deep emotional centre of the brain, has an important role during the dreaming stage of sleep. Good quality sleep creates a connection between the amygdala and the prefrontal cortex, the decision-making part of our brain. However, put sleep deprivation in the mix, and the link and connection is disrupted. Decision-making is compromised and emotional integrity can break down.

Numerous clinical observations demonstrate that mood and anxiety disorders co-occur with sleep disorders. In fact, mental health and lack of sleep are closely connected, with affected levels of stress hormones impacting critical thinking and emotional behaviour. This can have a detrimental impact on our relationships, our careers and our ability to lead a purposeful life.

WHAT IS THE SCIENCE BEHIND BETTER SLEEP?

Sleep can be an elusive creature for some of us but there are a few things we can be mindful of to increase the likelihood of good quality sleep. However, if you do think you have a sleep disorder such as sleep apnoea or insomnia, you might want to consider professional guidance or medical advice.

Set up a routine – Within our hypothalamus, a group of cells called the suprachiasmatic nucleus (SCN) respond to light and dark signals and control our circadian biological clock. The SCN will control hormone production and suppression affecting appetite, sleep drive, and body temperature. Our body clock expects routine. Try setting a 'go to bed' alarm and waking naturally – even on weekends and holidays.

Keep it dark – Melatonin is a brain hormone that helps regulate our circadian rhythm or sleep-wake cycle. The release of melatonin in the brain is heavily influenced by light stimulation of the retina. Try and stay away from bright lights or blue light created by screens before bed.

Get up if you can't fall asleep – If you are restless and can't fall asleep, get up from bed and do something different and relaxing. If we continue to stay in bed during this state, the brain will be conditioned to perceive bed as a place of interrupted sleep rather than good quality sleep. We need to reset and recondition the brain.

Keep cool - The body needs to drop core temperature by 1˚c to initiate, and stay, asleep. 18˚c is optimal for most people to get a good night's sleep. Another way to manufacture this temperature drop is by taking a warm bath to help dissipate heat and create drowsiness.

Alcohol and caffeine – Adenosine is a sleep factor and the stimulant effect of caffeine blocks the adenosine receptors in the brain. Caffeine is also known to interrupt our deep NREM sleep which can make us feel sleep deprived the next day. Alcohol can also be problematic because it acts like a sedative and slows down the brain, which interrupts the processes that occur in the brain during deep sleep. It has also been known to shorten REM sleep.

Naps - If you're feeling constantly tired on a daily basis, think about scheduling a 30 minute nap during the day. Studies show that napping for a short period of time, i.e. no more than 30 minutes, can restore alertness, and promote performance and learning.

IS IT TIME TO AWAKEN AND RECLAIM OUR RIGHT TO SLEEP?

Sleep is a fundamental biological process, and is essential to live a full and purposeful life. But why is sleep so misunderstood, and why do we still lack awareness of the full benefits? The fact that so many of us still take pride in losing sleep demonstrates this.

Sleep is something we do everyday, without question, reportedly for a third of our lives, and it's still a regular topic of conversation. Sleep has protective benefits but without it our physical and mental health are at stake.

Perhaps it's time to reclaim our right to sleep without the stigma of laziness. Just as we know that exercise, meditation and healthy eating are essential for good health, we must now put sleep back into that equation. You can reach for your pillow and sleep, guilt-free, knowing that the benefits of a good quality sleep will pay massive rewards and support your mental health, physical health, and wellbeing.

'Rest Deeply, Sleep Peacefully, Dream Sweetly.' ~ unknown

ABOUT THE AUTHOR

Tammy McPherson was born and raised in Australia and lives in the UK. She has dual Australian and British citizenship and still confuses her British peers with the occasional Australian colloquialism.

Her undergraduate studies and early career centred on public health and her first 'real' job was with a Non-Government Organisation based in the remote Kimberley region in Western Australia. She worked closely with the local communities on primary health initiatives.

From the remote shores of North-West Australia, she moved to London to travel and gain some life experience. There she undertook both a post graduate qualification in financial economics, and an M.B.A. Her career and study experiences took her from M&A projects to fintech.

Tammy has always had a love of 'all things science' and enjoys helping female students navigate STEM career choices.

Today, Tammy works with clients of a global investment management firm consulting on investment management solutions and exploring opportunities to develop partnerships. She is passionate about financial wellbeing and education.

Work/life balance immediately conjures the image of scales being, well, balanced. That's an over simplification of life. There are times when your work might need way more of your time and effort.

CAT MCMANUS

6 HOW GOOD IS THE OXYGEN IN YOUR MASK? (IN FACT, WHERE'S YOUR MASK?!)

So, we all know that faster, better, smarter results are good, right? We also know that we need to be purposeful in order to deliver our goals and objectives. We need to work hard.

We KNOW all this and we push, and push, and push to deliver in the ever-changing world we find ourselves in, where the pace of change is staggering and we have to run just to keep up. No wonder we're exhausted! If I work a bit harder, or perhaps a bit later, if I just do this one extra thing at the weekend, I'll get on top. Sound familiar?

If you're anything like me, you have a to-do list; it might be in your head, or written on scraps of paper, or be beautifully captured via some project management software or app. The thing is, the to-do list never ends! Something always lands on the top or bottom of it. I find myself having to call it a day and then start again the next day. I could conceivably work all night and the list would still be there! However, this chapter isn't about time management or to-do lists, it's about how we avoid burnout, and that we find the time to take the much needed, absolutely necessary and thoroughly deserved, break.

I'm one to talk! If you've ever done any type of personality test, I fall into the 'hyperachiever' category or the 'completer finisher.' I work hard and I'm pleased with my results. Oh, but I also pay the price! I'm much better than I was at managing my 'controller' and stress levels, but it's taken years of practice and lots of techniques. I want to share some of those with you, alongside some key concepts, so the long-term plan of looking after yourself will actually help you to achieve, and you'll feel happier in the process. Sound good?

First, let's get a couple of things straight. I don't want you to simply down tools and agree to work less or less hard. Remember, I'm a hyperachiever! That makes my eye twitch, and not in a good way. However, what I'd like you to think about is whether you have your work/life blend at the right levels. I have very purposefully not used the term work/life balance.

Work/life balance immediately conjures the image of scales being, well, balanced. That's an over simplification of life. There are times when your work might need way more of your time and effort. Perhaps you're a start-up, or about to close a big deal, or launch a new product. Naturally, you need to focus on work, and perhaps your own social time or family life will come second, at least for a while. Conversely, if you're starting a family, or someone is sick, or you're training for a marathon, you're going to be focussed on home and some things at work will take a backseat. These shifts in the 'balance' can happen within the working day, over several days, weeks, months or years. They might be project specific and time-bound, or a rolling issue with parameters not yet in place. All of this is ok. The point is, not only does work/life blend allow for this, it encourages it. All I'm asking now is whether it's working for you and did you choose it? I simply want you to be purposeful in your choices and decide if that is what your current situation needs. Is it what you want? You are master of your own destiny and if it isn't 'right', you can change it.

For now, let's continue with the concept of 'bandwidth'. We all have a certain amount of bandwidth and it can't be increased. You know the feeling when you just can't think about anything else because your brain is 'full'. If you are forced to consider other things, it's at the expense of something else. Something literally falls out of your brain to make room for the new thing that's presented itself. The more stress we have, the more deadlines there are, and the more on our to-do lists, coupled with family dynamics, and life in general, the harder it is to tune the bandwidth to areas of priority. We can get distracted with considerations that can wait, and we might miss the things that really need our attention. Short of being a practised Buddhist monk, or perhaps a Jedi Master, the only sure-fire way I know to prioritise the right things, is to step back. The analogy of not being able to see the wood for the trees is apt. When we're overloaded with items to process, we need time to declutter, free up some thinking space and then take appropriate and decisive action to move towards our goals, purposefully.

Well, this all sounds marvellous, but HOW do we do that? I'll get to that…stay with me.

Do you remember the game Buckaroo? It was an articulated plastic model of a mule named 'Roo'. The mule begins the game standing on all four feet, with a blanket on its back. Players take turns placing various items (e.g. saddle, cowboy hat, lantern, canteen, rope etc.) onto the mule's back, until one item causes the mule to buck up on its front legs, throwing off all the accumulated items.

So why am I reminding you of this 30-year-old childhood toy? It's because I want to give you a visual analogy of your bandwidth. There is only so much you can take before you 'buck'. This is not about an angry or physical response akin to Roo, the mental analogy works just as well. Life keeps putting items on you, and you'll recognise that a relatively small matter (item) is the one that tips the balance. It's disproportionate but it's the proverbial final straw. Your job now is to think about how close you are to the trigger at any given time, and to try and prevent the bucking from taking place. This isn't about learning to carry more weight. It's about taking some of the items off when you have the opportunity, so that when expected, or more likely, unexpected items get placed on, you have the headroom and capacity to deal with them, without everything flying off.

Now, let's talk buckets!

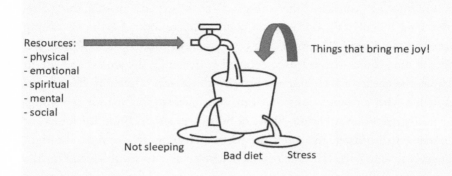

Resources:
- physical
- emotional
- spiritual
- mental
- social

Things that bring me joy!

Not sleeping

Bad diet   Stress

If you imagine your own joyful bucket – when it's full and brimming, you feel on top of the world, there isn't a mountain you can't climb. All your cylinders are firing, work doesn't even feel like work, you're on fire! Now imagine there's a hole in the bucket, and your joyfulness has been seeping out. Sometimes it drips out, sometimes it's gushing. Sometimes, it feels like someone kicked over your bucket and all your reserves washed away at once. What's important here is to be mindful about how full your bucket is at any given point. When it inevitably starts to deplete, you need measures in place to top it back up.

If you'd prefer, the bucket can be your heart. It's the inner sense of resilience and fortitude. It's what allows you to continue against inconceivable odds or hardship. It's the inner essence of you and what makes you smile. Your job is to keep this bucket (or your heart) as full as you can.

The concepts I've outlined so far lead us to the conclusion that we are only human, not goal crunching machines. To maintain a good output rate in the work sense, and also to enjoy the work/life blend we choose, requires effort to look after ourselves, and time to do just that.

Now some of you will be awful at this, others may be pretty good, whilst others may already do a fantastic job. For those of you who struggle, it might be because you consistently put others before yourself. This might be a spouse/ partner, child, family member, friend, colleague, staff or your boss. It can even be 'work' in the more general sense. Whilst this might seem like a positive attribute, it can lead to resentment, because deep down you realise that no-one is looking after YOU.

Have you heard the term 'wise-selfishness'? Immediately, you may be put off by the inclusion of the word 'selfish' – that's not supposed to be a good characteristic, right? Well no, not in the traditional sense, and I don't want to condone any lack of consideration for others, or suggest you should only be concerned with your own personal profit or pleasure. HOWEVER, if you're not ok, how will you continue to look out for those around you? If you continually put others before yourself, you'll inevitably reach a point where your own bucket is depleted. We all have a breaking point no matter what our levels of resilience, so you'll need to ensure you don't get to the bottom of your bucket.

The greatest analogy for wise-selfishness, as we're advised by the safety demonstrations on flights, is that you must put on your own oxygen mask before helping others. Imagine the scenario if you don't. If you didn't put on your mask first and went straight to helping others, you might 'save' those closest to you, maybe, but at what cost to yourself? If however, you put on your mask first and then set about helping those around you, you'd have a greater chance to save them and other people too.

Now, to the title of this chapter. How good is the oxygen in your mask? Let's imagine that you have control of the quality of the oxygen flowing to you. Imagine it was pure, filtered and of the highest grade - and it's pumped full of extra goodness. A secret sauce, putting the extra spring in your step or Va to your Voom!

The amazing thing is that YOU do have control over your oxygen supply, and it's all about what tops up your bucket and how you choose to look after yourself.

I work as a CEO/Senior Executive Coach, and have worked with high-integrity leaders on all the ideas and concepts outlined here. I've collated some of my favourite techniques and best practices for you to consider and decide which ones will work optimally for you.

I'll start with 'timeout'. I recommend taking a step back, whether in the moment or a longer break. This is crucial. It allows you to re-set, to reallocate work/life blend, bandwidth or at the very least, retune a little. By stepping back, you'll see where your efforts are best suited and where to put your energy and focus. This will lead to purposeful and impactful actions.

How: This will require you to schedule downtime and become better at building the concept of breaks into your life:

During the day – take a breath, take a walk, alarm your finish time for work, diary breakfast/lunch with the family or work colleagues, workout in the mornings, have time periods without meetings to get into work 'flow'. Change up the day and give your brain a chance to refresh.

Switch off in the evenings and at weekends – have a digital detox, reduce screen time, set min/max work hours if you have to work at all, have different rituals and routines so that your mind and body know it's not a workday e.g. a different breakfast or alarm time.

Book time off – once a month I like a 'sneaky day' – it's a day off for no reason other than to have a break from working, and I'm refreshed for the following day. Longer breaks might include a weekend away or a week/two-week holiday. Really give yourself time to step away – I bet you can think of examples in the past where this has presented a solution to a sticky problem, or you've come up with a brilliant idea. You just needed to give your brain the chance to think about it.

Tackling Stress. To appropriately prioritise and subsequently make the best decisions, you'll need to destress. Use timeout to mentally remove items that are taking you close to capacity – take them off your Buckaroo - build headroom back into your system so that you're good to go again on a whole new day/project/adventure.

How: Critically assess areas of your day/life that are building up negative feelings and emotions. Can you remove them or limit exposure to them? What actions would you need to take to do that?

Refocus and refresh. You'll do this by keeping your resilience bucket topped up. You'll feel less depleted and won't be making decisions on limited energy or resources. Instead, you'll be coming from a place of abundance, which will allow more innovation and creativity.

How: This means you need to know what causes your bucket to leak – you might not be able to plug all the holes, but if you know how to minimise the outflow, that's a start.

Consider what resources top you up – whether that's physical, emotional, spiritual, mental or social. How do you spend your time, who with and in what context? Also give consideration to sleep, nutrition and exercise. What do YOU need and are you getting enough? Write them down and see where gaps are appearing.

Then you'll need a list of things that make you smile, and give you joy – this is completely specific to you and there's no right or wrong. It can be a cheesy TV programme, baths, yoga, walks, particular foods, someone specific – it's not for anyone else to judge – you know what works for you!

Once you have all your lists – do them! Top up your joyful and resilience bucket as often as you can.

Look out for 'team you'. If you continually make sure your own oxygen mask is securely fastened then you'll be better placed to help those around you at home, work and in your community.

How: Acknowledge the concept of wise-selfishness is both smart and necessary. Don't feel guilty; know that it's helping those around you and will mean you don't burn out along the way. Plus, you'll be so much nicer to be around!

Spending time with friends and family is fabulous. It's certainly one of the ways I like to top up my own bucket. For a true sense of 'quiet' though, you might want to consider time alone. Time for self-reflection doesn't have to be a long time, but it's worth finding an hour here or there, to focus on what YOU really need.

Be kind to yourself. Empathy is a fabulous characteristic and one which all leadership frameworks champion. Ensure that not only are you displaying this worthy quality to those around you, but plenty is also being directed at yourself.

How: This requires positive self-talk and will help you maintain a positive mental attitude. It will give you permission to look after yourself, as well as working hard and striving for success. Enjoy the journey and not simply the destination.

Be compassionate to yourself and think about whether the ways your inner voice talks to you are appropriate. Learn when to turn up or quieten that voice – consider coaching or meditation to help with this.

Know what lights you up; a strong visual that makes you feel good, a morning mantra, a poem or song. Look at it, say it or listen to it, as often as you like!

Support. Looking out for 'team you' and taking care of yourself aren't always easy. I've already confessed to being rubbish! I have to really work hard to do the things I know are good for me. Consider expanding your team.

How: Have someone looking out for you – your very own 'health and wellbeing officer'. Someone who knows you well and ideally understands your priorities. It's not for them to decide what you should do. They are simply there to remind you of what you wanted to achieve and act as your accountability buddy. For this to work, you've got to be honest with them about where you're missing the mark. Whether they have coaching skills or not, talking will help you to work through your hurdles.

In the next chapter, Dom Hawes will take a closer look at how the people around you can affect your thinking and motivation, so who's on 'team you' is important.

What's next? Think about work/life blend and wise-selfishness, and decide how these concepts relate to you. I'd also like you to pick the visuals that work best for you – buckets, bandwidth and Buckaroo. You need to become good (or at least better) at realising when you're nearly 'full' or not full enough, and deploy all your appropriate countermeasures to get back on track.

Questions you can immediately ask yourself to get started:
- What's my current work/life blend – am I happy with that?
- What are my key stressors – am I able to reduce or remove them?
- What brings me joy – am I doing enough of that?
- How good is the oxygen in my mask?
- Who's on 'team me'?
- When was my last real downtime – when's my next?

We all need to re-set, re-balance and take care of ourselves. I want you to achieve any and all the goals you set for yourself, even if they might feel out of reach – I do love a Big Hairy Audacious Goal (BHAG)! What I don't want is for you to be so tired when you reach it/them that you fail to acknowledge the great achievement it is, or for you to have lost friends, relationships, health or purpose along the way.

Might you find me working at 8pm on a Friday night, you might. You might also find that I've shutdown the laptop, had a long walk to clear my head and shed the day, made some interesting food for dinner and settled down to read a good book or watch a new film release (or more likely an 80's classic!). What can I say, at least I'm aware of my bandwidth, stress levels and buckets these days – I'm a work in progress, just like you. I hope this has given you food for thought and may your Roo never buck!

To your success…….and a long and happy life.

ABOUT THE AUTHOR

With an extensive history in senior management roles in the biotech/pharmaceutical industry, as well as working in a wide range of organisations from start-ups to publicly-owned companies, Cat's driving passion is to see businesses reach their true potential, inspiring them to recognise that effective leadership is the key to achieving goals and 'blue skies' possibilities.

These roles provided her with invaluable experience in all aspects of business development; from understanding the complexities of venture capital and the business Angel community, to developing value growth propositions, business planning and preparing for investment or acquisition, including due diligence management.

Her position as the founder and Managing Director of a medical device company encouraged her entrepreneurial spirit to thrive.

Cat runs a well-established consultancy, specialising in business development and Intellectual Property management, working with companies in a range of roles, advising Board level management to deliver meaningful and commercially relevant results.

Her additional role as a Vistage Chair allows her to follow her passion, providing guidance, coaching and mentoring to local leaders, executives and growing businesses. Her Vistage Groups are underpinned by her firm belief that personal development, through continued learning, is the key driver to business success.

Living and working in Sheffield, UK, Cat enjoys hosting social gatherings with family and friends, but she's equally happy discovering new restaurants and sampling exciting cuisines. She is a self-confessed travel addict, especially if the destination allows indulgence in her love for skiing or ticking through her ever growing 'experience list.'

The human brain has evolved to protect us. When most of us think about the fight or flight mechanism of the brain's system, we think of snakes, tigers or spiders. These were existential threats when our species was evolving.

7

DOM HAWES
MAKERS AND TAKERS

I'm the guy who thought he'd sold a company, but ended up having to sell a house.

These days, I'm acutely aware of my shortcomings, but it wasn't always that way. Having stared into the business abyss, I came out of it knowing my purpose and being extremely comfortable both talking and writing about my failures. I still have plenty of failures to come, but each one teaches me something new.

In 2009, I thought I was pretty astute; on top of things; bullet proof. As it turns out, I wasn't that smart, and life decided to teach me a few lessons, the hard way. Years later, I've spent hundreds, if not thousands, of hours replaying what went wrong. Now, with the benefit of hindsight, I'm sharing the lessons learned with you.

Lesson one: the more you seek to boost your ego, the easier you'll fall prey to others and the farther you'll fall.

Lesson two: time seldom hides the truth, so if you are faking it, you'll be found wanting in time.

Lesson three: people that treat other people badly, but not you, just haven't got round to you yet.

Lesson four: listen: listen to the people you pay to advise you, or don't pay for their advice. Listen to your husband or wife. Listen to your gut. Listen to your senior team.

Lesson five: surround yourself with makers and avoid takers at all costs.

The bad decisions that led to losing the house weren't all mine, but they were my responsibility, and I am accountable because I trusted the wrong people. Worse, I did it against the advice of my wife, my lawyer, and my own gut feeling. I was easy prey because back then I was constantly seeking approval.

There was also significant pressure to change coming from colleagues, a rapidly changing market and, of course, there was a taker in the mix too. If you allow a taker into your life, they will take from you. It's as simple as that.

If I'd had a clearer sense of purpose and truly understood what mattered in business, I'd have done things differently. The failure might not have been prevented, because when there's a taker in the deal normal ethics are void, but at least I may have limited personal loss and protected at least some of our investment.

Nichola, my wife, was a victim in this. She warned me about the people I was dealing with. I already knew she was an excellent judge of character, but I did it anyway. When I had to sell the house, it was Nichola who kept a calm head and steered us through the mire. When I moved us 100 miles to a place she didn't want to live, she came anyway. My actions affected her deeply and I can't give back the four years it took us to recover.

Let's wind the clock back and I'll tell you how I ended up losing our house and what I learned.

In 2009, I was a 30% shareholder and managing director of an ecommerce wholesaler. We'd built it from scratch, backed by angel investors. We grew like stink pretty much from the off and we over-traded year after year, so found ourselves under-capitalised in a market that was changing fast around us. With excess stock and no ability (cash) to migrate our offering to meet new markets, our future was binary: either we raise more cash to fund change, or we sell the company.

Raising cash wasn't easy because it was 2009 and money was sparse, so a sale seemed our only option. But trade buyers in our market were conserving cash too because conditions were tough. Thus, without an investment to execute change and no buyer on the horizon, the company we'd fought hard to build looked in peril.

Then one evening, and I can still remember the moment as if it was yesterday, my Chairman told me he'd met with a business that might be interested in buying us. The firm was listed and would be using the acquisition of our business [and others] to raise new capital, which would give us much-needed investment. This excited me beyond belief.

Over the next few months, I got to know the acquirers. The principal was an extraordinarily aggressive individual. She seemed impressive and, as an excited party with an inflated opinion of himself, I ignored my gut and soaked up the fake praise.

The night before signing paperwork, I didn't sleep a wink. I knew something didn't add up, but I couldn't make sense of the feeling. With mixed support from our shareholders and against the advice of friends and a highly experienced commercial lawyer, I signed the deal.

A year and two months later, once the cash and life was sucked out of the business, and despite an agreement to fund the set up of our European operations, we were handed back the company. Supported by the Chairman, the acquisition was rescinded. Legal action seemed fruitless, so I took the punches, confessed to Nichola and we reluctantly placed our house on the market. Thankfully, it sold in time to meet the circling creditors' demands.

When things get bad as they often can in the life of an entrepreneur, there's only one question that matters: 'What's the worst that can happen?' In the pages of this book, there are tales of real life and death. For businesspeople, the worst is often less bad than you think. For their spouses? I can't answer that, but I think they have the worst scars.

The human brain has evolved to protect us. When most of us think about the fight or flight mechanism of the brain's system one[1], we think of snakes, tigers or spiders. These were existential threats when our species was evolving.

Today, while some people may face danger from wild animals or natures' anomalies, most of us don't. Our brains protect us from other threats. All we have to do is trust them. Gut instinct is your critical collection of heuristic defence mechanics and the most important of these, when it comes to people, is first impressions. Your senses are highly tuned to pick up all sorts of hidden signals from the very first time you meet a person. Trust them.

My single biggest mistake wasn't doing the deal, it was trusting a person my instinct, my wife and my lawyer were telling me not to trust. I ignored both what I was feeling and what those closest to me were telling me. Back then I was purposeless and naïve, but also blessed. Until that point, I was blessed to have been surrounded by good, honest people. Thus, I was naïve because I trusted everyone unless I had a reason not to, and even then, I was pretty forgiving. I was also purposeless, because my whole business existence was about seeking acceptance, rather than building something of value.

These days, I care much less what people think of me. I have a purpose and the good ones will be with me. When I set about creating my current business, very few people believed what I was trying to do was possible. Those that mattered did, and this time I listened to them, so I didn't give up. Through the experience that led me to loss, I learned that there are only two kinds of people in the business world. There are makers and takers. This time around, I'm axing takers as soon as I expose them.

Makers create value. They make things, they help people, they are inventors. Makers care about people. At the Royal Military Academy Sandhurst cadets are taught "Serve to Lead" as a mantra. It's the way makers operate. They use their skills and resources to help other people and, in the process, lead things in the right direction.

Takers destroy value. They take time, money and advantage of others. They help themselves. Takers are passengers; they don't care about people, only furthering their own agendas.

It was the descent into ruin that taught me this. Thereafter, it became my purpose to be a maker, and to get strong again so I could support others that want to make too.

Once it seemed to be commonly accepted that one needed to be tough in business. 'Nice people don't prosper,' they said. Well, that's not the case, and more and more people are starting to realise that.

In 1999, Catherine Ryan Hyde wrote the novel Pay it Forward. You may remember the movie, but it's the concept that's great. Instead of paying favours back, pay them forward by doing major favours for others, expecting no return other than passing on the generosity of action.

Here's an easy one you can do. The next time you see a helpless, homeless person on a cold, wet corner, go straight to the cash point and give them enough money to change their fortunes, if only for one day. Normally, that's the price of a hostel for the night, but if you can do more… do. It feels really good. Of course, you'll need to use your gut instinct to make sure you're not just aiding an addict, but there are scores and scores of well-deserving homeless on our streets. Use your judgement, help as often as you can, and I promise you'll feel fulfilment.

At work, being overtly kind and giving can be a little harder because acts of kindness, generosity, or humility can be taken advantage of by others. And here's the point. Evolution gave you gut instinct so you can work out who is a maker and who is a taker. Support makers and freeze out takers. Never, ever, ever do a deal with a taker. Don't engage with them, spend time with them or entertain any thought of changing them. Avoid them, and spend your considerable talents and precious time doing good for others who will do good.

The concept of paying it forward is catching on in business, because helping others to succeed at work isn't just kind and generous. Adam Grant, Professor of Management and Psychology at Wharton Business School, based his 2013 best-selling business book "Give and Take" on his own research (givers and takers are the same thing as makers and takers).

In his 2016 Ted@IBM talk, Adam Grant explained: 'Takers are self-serving in their interactions. It's all about what can you do for me. The opposite is a giver. It's somebody who approaches most interactions by asking, what can I do for you?'

He then explains that in reality most people are not strictly one or the other, they're a little of both most of the time – or a matcher. This is where my experience and opinion and his research diverge a little. I believe that people are predominantly one thing or the other, not both. It might be that I'm wrong in this, but if more of us consciously set out to be makers or givers, not only would our world be nicer, we'd all be more successful too. If in doubt, give.

Grant continued to explain that givers make their organisations better too. It turns out that givers foster a culture that is more collaborative, more profitable, more enjoyable for employees, and more highly rated by customers too. Giving works.

Giving isn't hard at all. And I'm not for one moment suggesting you give away everything you've earned. But if you concentrate on being a maker and avoid takers at all costs, you'll be happier, more successful and probably better off in the long run too.

I didn't lose my house by giving. I lost it because a taker took money, time and trust from me. But I have the last laugh. If I hadn't lived through loss, I wouldn't have experienced the things that have brought me to today. I wouldn't have the drive to start the business I did in 2018 which, two years later, comprises 65 makers. Next year, we'll be 200 and we're using the power of all those people to support and help businesses to beat businesses that take.

I'm the guy who thought he'd sold a company but ended up having to sell his family's house.

I'm the guy who started another company. It's better than the old one and it's going to change the world. Look me up. I need all the makers I can muster.

ENDNOTES

1   Reference Daniel Kahnemann

ABOUT THE AUTHOR

Dom Hawes' career has been varied, but a love of marketing, strategy and deal-making has provided the thread that has guided his development. He is currently CEO of marketing services group, Selbey Anderson.

After a short and unsuccessful stint at university, Dom joined the British Army and was commissioned into the Blues and Royals. After completing five years' service as an officer, he executed a transition into the creative services industry, starting as a junior account executive at a London PR company.

Over the next six years, Dom worked his way up the marketing tree ending his agency experience as a marketing consultant with a leading digital and design agency. He left the agency world to join a tech start-up and, from there, joined an early-stage investment company as their VP Marketing, where he launched 16 businesses before leaving to start his own venture.

Between 2001 and 2009 Dom co-founded, built and ultimately sold a product company and ecommerce wholesaler. If you've read this chapter, you'll know how well that went!

In 2012, after Dom sold the family house and he, his wife Nichola and their vizsla, Dixie, moved to rural Leicestershire to lick wounds, seek mojo and plan a comeback.

Dom is an optimist and has always had a near unshakable belief in the ability of others. The experience he shared so candidly in his chapter was a watershed moment in his life, which led to a realisation that it's not ok just to muddle through.

It took five years of soul searching to find his purpose but find it he did.

These days, Dom lives with his family close to the banks of the river Great Ouse in Bedford where he enjoys his other great passion, rowing. Dom is a five-time British Rowing Masters National Champion and, as a member of the Bedford Star Masters' squad, has won gold medals at both European and World Masters regattas.

In 2018, he co-founded Selbey Anderson which, since commencing trading in 2019, has grown in 24 months to just under 100 people with revenues of £9.5m (35 more since writing his chapter). The group's trajectory continues to rise.

'When Chris explained the concept for this book, I knew I wanted to take part.' Dom explains, 'It's no coincidence that the extraordinary success of the squad on the water has coincided with my group's success off it. In both worlds I've been able to live my new purpose of giving to get. In the boat, I've been led by and learned a great deal from an amazing athlete called Kevan Armstrong. He's one of the most extraordinary makers I've ever met. At work, I'm building a team made up exclusively of makers. Together, we're giving a lot and we'll all get what we deserve too, I hope - happiness, fulfilment and a great deal of fun along the way.'

Every day we have to make decisions; what to have for breakfast or moving countries. When choosing one over another, we shape our lives. This process of decision-making can be empowering and allows us to have many benefits, most importantly self-determination. However, it can also bring anxiety, regret, and frustration, as it forces us to face the inner conflict around the possibility of dissatisfaction and the 'wrong' decision - back to the start-stop internal conversation.

ADAM HARRIS

MIND THE MIND

8

Imposter syndrome, self-limiting beliefs, mental models, comparing ourselves and decision-making paralysis

The aspect of the mind, how we think, who we are, what we are and why we are here…these are all questions that I ask myself on a weekly, daily, and often moment by moment basis. I heard a phrase many years ago, 'our thoughts are only our thoughts unless verbalised or written down.' How often do we get caught, denied, or suppressed by our own mind? For me this is a daily excursion into the life and wonder of our sub-conscious and mind. Those that know me would be surprised to realise my over-analysing of everything I do, think or say; the inner critic, the chimp, the shadow and many other terms are used, depending on who you read. For me, this 'imposter syndrome' is something, a part of me, someone who shows up at various points and in varying outfits with a degree of messages, depending on whether it wants to support me or hinder me, and can flip and change in a split second. Growing up, I found myself inquisitive, challenging norms and the status quo. This proved to be quite confrontational for many in my life. I had a thirst, an intrigue to understand. In some ways my 'imposter' had no filter, and I was always probing and prodding to find the answers others couldn't give me. I found myself isolated and often on my own; something as time has passed me by, I have learned to embrace and love.

I found in my early years, and subsequently as a coach, that before making a decision we have to release our fear of making a wrong decision. This often is referred to as 'decision paralysis.' The fear of the unknown is worse than the position we are starting from, and in order to start something, we have to stop something. Recently myself and my family moved from a 'comfortable' state of being in the UK, to NZ, on the other side of the world, to an area that we had never been, to a brand new school, with a brand new methodology of learning. With it has come change, challenge and growth – all of which are still continuing and at times have been incredibly difficult. The 'imposter' within me refers back to a time and place when things were easier, in all aspects of being. So how/what do I say to the 'imposter' that keeps trying to pull me down, back into the swamp, the valley, the pit of despair?

I remember having a conversation with my youngest daughter who was 6 at the time and talking about our inner voice/monologue. The relief on her face was a true moment of 'energetic release' when she said, 'you have someone that talks to you as well?' Having just finished some work with Professor Srikumar Rao, who subsequently became a friend and mentor, I have asked the question to leadership teams, 'Put your hand up if you have conversations with yourself in your head?' To which ½ - ¾ put their hands up. 'And to those of you that didn't put your hand up, did you ask yourself the question?' That's your inner voice, or as Dr. Rao describes it, mental chatter.

What is mental chatter? It is the monologue that we have going on in our heads - all the time.

You might say, it's the narrator of the movie that we are constantly watching in our minds. It's the voice of commentary, judgement and worry— attempting to control the future, avert disaster, and steer you through the world. Is your mental chatter taking you to a place where you are upbeat, energised, optimistic about the future and full of beans? Or, is it taking you to a dark place of foreboding, anxiety, fear of the future and insecurity about what will happen to you?

For many, understanding and learning how to listen and observe, is a challenge they never get to. After all who discusses it? It's not a conversation for the dinner table. Or is it? More recently the concept of mindfulness and meditation has become widely accepted. When doing meditation, being 'still' allows you to silence the mental chatter and just 'be' in the moment and present. How, and what do you do, to 'be' in the moment, to be in flow? When you're that still and calm, or in complete flow, your mental chatter is silenced and the 'imposter' is completely in check.

Every day we have to make decisions; what to have for breakfast or moving countries. When choosing one over another, we shape our lives. This process of decision-making can be empowering and allows us to have many benefits, most importantly self-determination. However, it can also bring anxiety, regret, and frustration, as it forces us to face the inner conflict around the possibility of dissatisfaction and the 'wrong' decision - back to the start-stop internal conversation. Often, we look to those closest to us, giving them permission and granting them ownership of the decision, while dissolving responsibility and paralysing ourselves from making the decision. The more comfortable we become in being uncomfortable with our decisions, allows us to grow more self-sufficient, confident, and secure that we are able to trust ourselves to make the 'choice.' It's like a muscle, we have to train it to use it. Deciding to do something, even if it's doing nothing, allows our 'imposter' to be kept quiet, while we listen, learn and gather information to make a decision.

You don't have to play golf to understand the following metaphor, so imagine you're on the 1st Tee. You can see the hole in the distance down and to the left. You look at the scene in front of you; you have the green, the rough, the trees. You have the hazards with the water and the bunkers, as well as some hills. You then see what the weather is doing, which way the wind is blowing and how fast. You look in your bag. Do you pick a wood to go long, or do you pick an iron to come up short with more precision? You take your time to decide. You pick your club, have a number of swings to practice, and look at those you're playing to see what they have done, and potentially feel the pressure of expectation on yourself, as well as from others. Sometimes the most important thing to do is 'HIT THE BALL'. At least by doing so we are now moving, and gathering some momentum, as Mark E Smith from Inspiral Carpets sang in the 70's, 'no one ever said it was going to be easy'.

Owning our decisions, good or bad, for me is part of the challenge. Things won't go the way we expect them to, but if we are able to do them for the right reasons, and the right times – why do we allow the fear of the unknown, the 'imposter' within us, to take control? We each have the power to affect our daily life and our long-term well-being. We are already doing it subconsciously in our life to exist and survive. Within us, is the power to process and weigh up the decision, looking at the positives and negatives. Our intuition and inner wisdom is there; we have to find a way of trying to decipher the 'imposter,' to allow us to have clarity without judgement, and accept and respect the decisions we make. Often our ability to get guidance and suggestions from others is to reinforce what we already know. Giving ourselves permission to release the fear of the wrong decision, will allow us the ability to make 'a' decision and 'hit the ball'. Our perception of eventualities is often set on a mental model that is created for the 'perfect' outcome. Often unexpected paths are created by the seemingly wrong decision, as destiny takes a different course. Are you doing and living your life exactly the way you planned it? The nuances and differences to the 'plan' are where the surprises come from. This is highlighted in a story I often share, 'Good thing, bad thing, who knows?'

Owning our choices allows us to be accepting of the eventuality of the outcomes. Our decision is a reflection of our creativity, our awareness, our power, and our ability to move towards or away from something - stopping something in order to start something. Consciously owning and taking responsibility for our decisions, allows us to make informed choices, leading us to live with a sense of being 'Frank and Fearless' for ourselves, creating freedom, focus, and flow in our life.

You have probably heard the phrase 'everything happens for a reason' and nothing is either good or bad, but our thinking makes it so. One of my favourite mental models illustrates ancient wisdom to reserve judgement; to remain in the present moment; to mitigate undue stress and worry; to avoid panic; and to have the courage to be moved forward regardless. This is called 'Good thing? Bad thing? Who knows?'

SECRET OF JOY?

Once upon a time, an old farmer lived in a valley with his son, a handsome and dutiful youth. They lived a peaceful life despite a lack of material possessions. They were very happy. So much so, that neighbours began to get envious and wanted to understand the secret of their happiness.

SAVINGS AND LOSS?

One day, the old man used all his savings to buy a young and beautiful horse. The very same day he bought it, the horse jumped the fence and escaped into the hills. The neighbours came to express their concern, 'Oh, that's too bad. How are you going to work the fields now?'

The farmer replied, 'Good thing? Bad thing? Who knows?'

DOUBLE FORTUNE?

In a few days, his horse came back from the hills and brought ten fine horses with him. The neighbours again gathered around, 'Oh, how lucky! Now you can do much more work than ever before!' they said.

The farmer replied, 'Good thing? Bad thing? Who knows?'

MISFORTUNE?

The next day, the farmer's son fell off one of the new horses and broke his leg. 'Such misfortune,' said the neighbours. The leg healed crookedly and left the son with a permanent limp and endless pain. The neighbours were concerned again, 'Now that he is incapacitated, he can't help you around, that's too bad.'

The farmer replied, 'Good thing? Bad thing? Who knows?'

TRAGEDY?

Soon, the news came that war had broken out, and all the young men were required to join the army. The villagers were sad because they knew that many of the young men will not come back. The farmer's son could not be drafted because of his broken leg. His neighbours were envious: 'How lucky! You get to keep your only son!'

The farmer replied, 'Good thing? Bad thing? Who knows?'

And the narrative goes on …

CONCLUSION

Life will happen and continue evolving regardless. Things may seem bad, they may seem good, only time will tell. What if we can alter our perception in the moment, toward believing that there is a perfect reason for the way in which the universe is unfolding the way it is?

In a nutshell, everything that seems on the surface to be bad may be good in disguise. And everything that seems good on the surface may not always be so.

What would life be like without our perception, our in-moment judgements and negative narratives, or the internal 'imposter syndrome' and how it takes over our thoughts? We may not be conscious that we are looking at everything from a narrow viewpoint in doing so, but from the higher perspective, what appears tragic can be the most appropriate way forward.

Why do we compare ourselves to others? The time to stop is now! Another phrase I heard long ago 'if you're going to compare some of yourself compare all of yourself.' When we look at someone else and 'want' or sometimes 'don't want' for what they have, or don't have in their life, we are focused on one individual item or experience. We have no idea what has happened to get to that point, or the other aspects that are influencing and affecting their lives.

Everyone else is taken, there is nobody else like YOU in the world. Is this not worth celebrating instead of the 'imposter' comparing or picking faults in what you don't have or are yet to achieve? Our uniqueness, the difference, is what we should acknowledge, yet we are often pulled towards images or expectations of what others are, or are not.

As human nature dictates, we want to compare ourselves to others and see how we 'stack' up, emphasised if we have a perception that others are better than us, or have something we want. Comparing ourselves with others is a waste of time because there is no one like us and this makes us incomparable. It is often easier to look at others and outside of ourselves, and compare to other people, rather than owning our life and taking responsibility for our progress toward fulfilment and our life's purpose. The courage comes from self-reflecting and looking at how we measure up against our potential and the standards we expect and set for ourselves.

Each of us is unique with different reasons for existing, expectations, and life purpose to fulfil, and learning how we navigate through this is challenging. If it were easy, we would already have done it. Comparing our lives to others when we don't know what they are here to learn or fulfil, doesn't benefit us or serve us. When we can find permission, and an ability to accept ourselves, understand our gifts, our talents, and qualities that we alone own, we focus within instead of outwardly. One thing that has helped me is 'Clifton Strengths Finder,' from Gallup and Tom Rath, based on the work of Donald O. Clifton, which I now use with people I work with. Another phrase, 'work to your strengths, manage your weaknesses,' goes along with, 'surround yourself with people who are better than you.' When we do this and are able to work in the space that we both love, and we excel at working on our 'A' game, this can allow us to become a force of nature, as we get into 'flow' and time has a habit of just disappearing. Realising our value, our uniqueness, enables us to bring the best of ourselves so we can 'thrive with purpose,' rather than become preoccupied with our 'imposter,' meaninglessly comparing ourselves to others.

As you are reading this, I'm sure you're thinking of aspects, moments in time, life events, even something that is happening now, that with hindsight, a change of an angle, a turn of the kaleidoscope, may have changed your view, your opinion, your perception, or your reaction.

As we take ownership of our thoughts, we begin to lead our mind and own our decisions, as opposed to our mind owning and leading us. As we lead ourselves, we begin to have the space and capacity to lead others.

ABOUT THE AUTHOR

Adam Harris is a serial and (often) successful business leader, author, and innovator, with a keen understanding of the value of strategic connections and an equally ardent aversion to clutter, noise, fluff, and the drudgery that gets in the way of our success. As The Introducer, he seeks to acquaint us not only with the power of networks, but with enhanced results and greater opportunity.

Adam established his business consultancy, Fresh Mindset by The Introducer, in 2010, and has worked with CEOs and senior managers providing training, coaching and high-level peer group activities to convert opportunities into successes, drive profit, facilitate change, define company direction and leverage the network.

He uses the 'Frank & Fearless - grab the bull by the horns' approach to board leadership.

Adam takes action with services that increase the effectiveness of your board communication and leadership. Speak freely, clearly and constructively to move your business forwards, together.

- Board Chair
- Board Training
- Coaching

Along with Robert Craven, he is the co-author of the book 'Check-in Strategy Journal.'
www.checkinjournal.com/adam-harris

- Virtual + Remote Leader and CEO Coach
- EOS Implementer
- IT in Business, IT Resellers, IT Channel Community
- Technology commentator
- Professional introducer and facilitator
- Trusted Advisor, Coach, Mentor, Confidant, Strategist
- Team Leader
- Author
- Chair Vistage International
- Creative Counsel and Speaker

Adam lives in Taranaki, New Zealand, with his wife and two small daughters, who keep him well and truly on his toes. Well-travelled, and a lover of American football, he is an improvised comedy performer and health regime convert. Adam combines all his passions into his work, his home life and his diverse interests.

http://www.fresh-mindset.co.uk/

https://frankandfearless.com/

My fellow officer cadets and I knew ....
the different stressors that could elicit
an angry outburst or tears.... (but)
we didn't even know first names....
Eventually the desire to make that
human connection took over and we
made the time to learn these 'little
things' about one another.

9

KATE PHILP
LEADERSHIP BY LITTLE THINGS

A little thank you goes a long way. This simple, but powerful piece of advice is one of the earliest guiding principles that my mum taught me. It forms the foundation of my approach to leadership, which I am exploring in this chapter through the lens of 'the every day' – not in crisis situations, not through a period of change, but 'normal' (whatever that means to you), daily life.

I am a fan of the practical, understanding how great wisdom can be turned into great action; asking the 'so what?' question that tries to make the link between the two. This is by no means easy, so I'm starting simply, looking at some of the little ways you can demonstrate leadership, with the aim of sharing advice I have taken and experience I have gained. After all, 'a muscle has to be exercised 1,000 times for the movement to become learned'[1], so simple is good. I will draw upon the research and reflections of internationally acclaimed organisations and leaders, but my 'go to' when it comes to role models, are the people I know (and often love).

Let's start with Mum, which seems appropriate given she was at my start! Mum is an incredible 'people person' whose empathy and curiosity know no bounds. I can't dress it up and I wouldn't want to; as well as being a fan of 'little things', I also commend simplicity. I love language (being a classicist you might expect nothing less), so I enjoy the artistry that writers and poets employ to demonstrate the clever and complex ways of creating their art, but I think the 'product', the 'creation', should still be simple in its message, accessible to all.

'A little thank you goes a long way' is a great example of what I mean by 'Leadership By Little Things'. To thank someone, you have to have awareness of who they are and what they have done; the effect this has had on you or how their actions have made a difference to you; the positive intention of wanting to give them recognition for this; and the decision how best to do it based either on what suits you best[2], and/or what will mean the most to them.

This makes the simple act of thanking someone seem rather complex. This is not my intent, rather it is to demonstrate how powerful this simple act can be, *because of all that it comprises,* and therefore the disproportionate impact it can have. To some, like my mum, this act will come naturally; for others, I believe it can be learned, but remember it needs to be practised. You might pick it up sooner than 1,000 repetitions, but if not, you'll have made a lot of people feel appreciated!

KNOW YOUR PEOPLE AS PEOPLE

During my year at Sandhurst[3], I learned a lot about the true meaning of teamwork; the ability to work together in pursuit of a common goal, despite any personal differences. My fellow officer cadets and I knew how we each fared when sleep-deprived, who performed better 'in the field', and the different stressors that could elicit an angry outburst or tears. We knew all this before knowing where each of us was from, whether we had siblings or had been to university, and what interests we had. We didn't even know first names, since only surnames were used. Undoubtedly, this set us up well when working in a high-pressure environment, but it wasn't enough for sustainable relationships. Eventually the desire to make that human connection took over and we made the time to learn these 'little things' about one another.

Why does it matter to know somebody's family background, the sports teams or charities they support, and whether they have a favourite drink or travel destination? There are 'big' reasons (in a 'Maslow's hierarchy of needs' context) to do with better understanding their culture, values and commitments outside of work (psychological needs), and the 'smaller' ones, to do with their interests and what gives them pleasure (self-fulfilment needs).

'Maslow's hierarchy of needs'[x].

As a leader you can draw on both of these: a good grasp of the former helps you to understand why a colleague (or friend) is not handling pressure well at a particular time, for example, because their first child has just started school, or they are caring for an elderly relative. Taking the time to gather information on the latter means that you can refer to how their sports team fared at the weekend, or recommend a book or documentary on their favourite country.

These small acts show that you have bothered to find out the information, you've retained it, thought about it outside of the work environment, and found an opportunity to re-engage in that conversation. How you choose to do so is down to personal style and knowledge of the person concerned; you can commiserate a team's defeat, or you can use it as an opportunity to 'banter' with them.

WALK THE WALK

When I joined my first regiment, the senior subaltern (the longest serving lieutenant, closest to promotion to captain), offered me the following advice: 'Whenever you have something you wish to discuss with someone, do it face to face as often as you can, rather than over the phone.' In 2003, email was not universal in the army, hence this form of communication wasn't even mentioned – bliss, I hear some of you cry!

This guidance not only aided my fitness by walking or cycling around camp, it also improved my ability to prioritise, delegate and use my initiative; working out what didn't need to be dealt with straightaway, what didn't need to be dealt with by me, and what I could deal with under my own steam. And it earned me a good reputation, especially amongst the LE officers[5] who themselves would have spent years running around camp. I think it offered them respect, and as a result they were always willing to give me their time, advice and practical help.

Reflecting on this, I feel I had a different relationship with the LE cohort in my second regiment where, now a captain, I was busier and carried greater responsibility. The provision of email (something I'd naively craved in my first posting), lulled me into the territory of electronic communication as my primary means of 'doing business', where all too often we think that our responsibility for a task disappears as soon as we hit the 'send' button. Had I balanced this better with more face-to-face conversations, I believe I would have developed stronger relationships.

So why didn't I continue the good practice I'd proven had worked in my first regiment? I'm sure some of it was down to a genuine belief that I was too busy (something I now raise an eyebrow at), but I fear a part of me, at least, believed I'd earned the right not to have to tread the ground as I had as a subaltern. It makes me recoil a little to admit that lack of humility, a quality I believe in fiercely, but sometimes it is natural to feel that you have been through a rite of passage and can now enjoy whatever benefit it has gained for you. As with so many things, I believe it is a matter of balance. Enjoy the benefit, but don't dismiss the behaviour that earned it for you. If you believe in leading by example, you still have to exemplify the behaviour. You still have to walk the walk.

I understand that it isn't always practical or possible to have an 'in the flesh' discussion, but something that the Covid-19 pandemic has taught us is that much more can be done virtually than we ever believed possible. Whilst this isn't the same as being in the same room with someone, it offers some of the benefits: it demonstrates respect that you can be bothered to talk the matter through rather than abrogate responsibility by handing it off in an email; it encourages you to prioritise and organise your work so that you can cover multiple issues in one conversation; and it creates the opportunity to check in with them on a personal level. You can glean so much more about how a person is feeling when you see them as well as speak to them. Of course, it is wise to consider what another person's preference is. Do they prefer operating electronically, for example? Even asking that question shows empathy that is itself, a 'little' demonstration of leadership.

This 'Leadership By Little Things' is an approach I have referred to often in my speaking work, but I've been hesitant to elevate to a topic in its own right, questioning whether it is too small, too simple, too obvious. Seeking reassurance, therefore, I did two things: I asked a couple of friends for their opinions[6], and I searched for examples of organisations and leaders who have demonstrated this approach. The former gave me a hearty and excited thumbs up, coupled with their own examples of how they, or others they know, have exercised leadership in 'little' ways.

KINDNESS

'Kindness' seems to be an over-arching term that encapsulates this approach for many, and it is a word that I have become more comfortable with as I have matured. The young army officer, whilst never intentionally unkind, would not have considered kindness to be an important quality, fearing the accusation of 'weakness' that might follow. But I am a firm believer in leadership starting with self, and through counselling support I have recognised the importance of self-care, being kind to yourself and not judging yourself too harshly. So I am now an advocate of kindness in leadership, which doesn't preclude disagreement or challenge, but does place emphasis on creating the safe space to do so, which Chris Paton will expand on in chapter 15.

BENDING THE RULES

'Bending the rules' also emerged as one of the informal ways a leader can look after their people; it relies on courage to face challenge from those who are bent on upholding the rules, as well as knowing that the beneficiary of your 'flexibility' won't take advantage. Clear communication, expectation management and robustness are critical. It is not an easy approach to practise, but it can yield strong and enduring loyalty as well as, sometimes, simply being the right thing to do. I adopted this approach on my tour of Afghanistan when I gave permission for one of my team to have an extended period of R&R[7] to incorporate an additional week of paternity leave. The Brigade policy on tour was not to award any paternity leave, but I knew the personal circumstances of this soldier and believed he and his wife would benefit more from his presence than my team, and our ability to do our job would suffer from his absence. I was verbally disciplined for my decision, but no formal action was taken, and I remembered the advice of my first boss: 'Better to seek forgiveness than ask permission.' Brave words, but a strong demonstration of the trust he placed in me, which years later, undoubtedly gave me the courage to do what I felt was right for my soldier.

One of these friends recommended I look up Sir Ken Robinson, an educator and bestselling author with a passion for creative and cultural education. Sir Ken sadly died in August 2020, but his legacy is strong. His TED talk, 'Do Schools Kill Creativity?' is the most watched in TED's history, having been viewed online over 60 million times and seen by an estimated 380 million people in 160 countries[8]. His talks are lively and passionate, his key points illustrated by stories that are funny, touching and insightful.

One such example is that of a young girl in the 1930s who was taken to see a doctor because of her seeming inability to engage with anything in school. The doctor noticed that she sat on her hands throughout the 20 minutes that he spoke with her mother, so he engineered a reason to leave her in the room on her own, but turned on the radio before he and the girl's mother left. They watched her get up and dance with wild abandon and the doctor pronounced his diagnosis: 'Gillian isn't sick….she's a dancer. Take her to a dance school.'[9] This was Dame Gillian Lynne DBE, a multimillionaire former member of the Royal Ballet, choreographer of 'Cats' and 'Phantom of the Opera', among others.

My interest in this story is less the recognition that intelligence includes creativity, and more the action of the doctor, who *noticed* something as small and seemingly insignificant as Gillian sitting on her hands, a 'little' thing that changed her life.

The importance of paying attention to 'little things' reminds me of Sir Dave Brailsford's concept of 'marginal gains', which the former Performance Director at British Cycling applied to improve the team's performance, by breaking down the action of riding a bike into its component parts and improving each by 1%. The desired outcome in the case of British Cycling was to improve performance; when it comes to leadership, my aim is to open the eyes of the leader to the whole person. This is a similar strategy to Sir Dave's in its holistic nature, with improved performance usually happening as a result.

This whole person approach was incorporated into Google's people management practices, after it experimented with having no managers at all. This was part of its review of whether managers matter in an engineering organisation, with a Human Resources strategy focused on data[10]. Its research project, 'Project Oxygen', measured key management behaviours and their impact. The results showed that good managers do matter but stressed the importance of balance; sufficient management to prevent small personal issues being elevated to the CEO, but not so much as to be stifling. Eight traits were identified that the most effective managers share, these four in particular resonate with the whole person approach:

A good manager:
- Is a good coach
- Expresses interest in and concern for team members' success and personal wellbeing
- Is a good communicator – listens and shares information
- Helps with career development

Garvin neatly summarises this, describing how managers 'must go beyond overseeing the day-to-day work and support their employees' personal needs, development, and career planning.'[11]

My penultimate reference, which I think encapsulates walking the walk of the people-centred approach through a little thank you, is the practice of the former US President, Barack Obama. He personally answered ten letters from members of the public, every night of his presidency. To my knowledge, nothing was made of this during his tenure, the anecdote has come out in both his and Michelle's autobiographies.

Making a human connection, in whatever way you can, is perhaps at the heart of this chapter. For those who prefer a more down-to-earth example, I turn to the late Lieutenant Colonel Henry Worsley OBE, whose talk in 2013 at the Royal Geographical Society formed part of my own preparations for an expedition to Antarctica. In response to my question about how best to prepare, Col Henry, without hesitation, said: 'Work out what irritates you about each person, then let it go.' A clear message from a courageous man with a big heart; themes that Kate Marshall will expand on in the next chapter.

ENDNOTES

1   According to one of my Rehabilitation Instructors at the Defence Medical Rehabilitation Centre, Headley Court.

2   In terms of your style and the practicalities of your situation – are you co-located so that you can deliver the thank you in person, or will the written word or a phone call make more sense?

3   The Royal Military Academy Sandhurst (RMAS) where, if you are joining the army as an officer, you spend your first year of training.

4   www.simplypsychology.org.

5   Late Entry (LE) officers are those who have served 22 years as a soldier before being commissioned.

6   As I mentioned earlier, the opinions I respect the most tend to be those of people I know.

7   Rest and recuperation (R&R): a period of leave, usually 2 weeks, for every personnel deployed on a 6-month operational tour.

8   http://www.sirkenrobinson.com.

9   Melanie Curtin, Feb 28, 2018, http://www.inc.com.

10   David A. Garvin: 'How Google Sold Its Engineers On Management', Harvard Business Review, Dec 2013, Vol. 91 Issue 12, p74-82.

11   Ibid., 82.

ABOUT THE AUTHOR

Joining the Army after graduating in Classics from Oxford University, Kate was deployed on operations in Iraq and Afghanistan, where her leadership, decision-making, technical skill and adaptability were brutally tested in the fast-paced environment of front-line operations. Kate's tour of Afghanistan came to an abrupt end when injuries caused by an Improvised Explosive Device (IED) resulted in her electing to have her leg amputated below the knee, becoming the first British female to lose a limb in combat.

Persistent medical issues demanded further surgery and that she re-focus her rehab with a new goal. In 2013 Kate trekked to the South Pole as part of an expedition organised by the charity Walking With The Wounded. This earned her the honour of being shortlisted in the 'Women of the Year' awards in 2014.

Leaving the Army after 13 years service, Kate now works as a Coach and Speaker, bringing her love of developing soldiers into the civilian world. Drawing on her military experience in leadership, communication, relationship management and providing solutions under pressure, as well as lessons in resilience and managing uncertainty learned from dealing with a life-changing injury, Kate thrives on helping clients clarify challenges and seek collaborative solutions. She is comfortable working at multiple levels and has experience in a variety of sectors including legal, financial services, insurance, construction, healthcare, media, hospitality and education.

Balancing an eye for detail with the big picture, and a ready ability to switch focus between people and task, Kate supports people who are 'stuck' and want to move forward, by opening possibilities to create choice. Taking her own medicine, Kate jumped at the opportunity to move into the writing world and feels her chapter matches the challenge: 'I've written about something I've long believed in – the importance of the little actions we take – and I've been able to do so in a small way, with just a single chapter. The daunting prospect of writing a book might have kept me stuck in the 'wannabe writer' zone so I'm grateful for this opportunity. I've loved the experience and am delighted to be part of a great team with a strong purpose.'

Kate holds a CMI Level 7 Extended Diploma in Strategic Management & Leadership, a Diploma in Life & Business Coaching accredited by the

Association for Coaching, and is an NLP Practitioner.

Outside of work, Kate continues her love of exercise, running when her leg permits it and volunteering at her local parkrun; you can hear her talk enthusiastically about this on the Free Weekly Timed podcast. Her two springer spaniels also help to keep her fit but sadly are not as well-disciplined as her soldiers! Kate is also honoured to be an ambassador for ABF, The Soldier's Charity and a trustee of the Black Stork Charity responsible for building the £300 million defence rehabilitation facility at Stanford Hall, as part of the Defence and National Rehabilitation Centre.

When you have too much fear in a system, you create fog. Fog in an organisation or relationship causes exactly the same response as experiencing fog when you are driving the car. You slow down, you hold tension in your body, you narrow your focus – you lack clarity.

10

KATE MARSHALL

HEAD AND HEART COURAGEOUS LEADERSHIP

Who are you? This is the question I ask at the beginning of my work with leaders, and often it seems to create great anxiety or even confusion. Of course, who we are isn't defined by who we say we are, it's defined by how others experience us.

But really who are you? Who have you become?

I was the youngest of four children with a significant gap between my elder brother and sister and my immediate sister who is two years older than me. We had a happy but busy home with my parents running a number of small businesses, and we lived on a farm. My earliest memories are being with them in their businesses, helping out as a small child, being around them as they worked. All the while I craved their attention and found if I was resourceful, and found ways to make their lives easier, I got that attention. They were the old-fashioned parents where affection was not overtly demonstrated, yet I knew I was loved. In many ways I had to grow up pretty quickly, I was left to my own devices a lot and that created a very strong sense of independence, and also a strong work ethic. When I was 17, I left school to work in Manchester and very quickly realised that wasn't adventurous enough; I wanted to explore America. Off I went, barely 18 with little money, very few qualifications and big ambition. I had very little except a true belief that I would work it out – I always had!

My stay in USA only lasted a year as I missed home, and when I returned at age 19 ½, I immediately found work as an assistant buyer in a department store, with my passion for hard work and a belief that I could work things out. By age 23, I was running the business which had 70 staff and was the 2nd most profitable in the chain across the UK.

You see my early childhood taught me, if you want something to happen you need to make it happen, don't wait for others to show the way. It taught me self-leadership. That has given me a very strong work ethic, which I am grateful for…it's also a problem. I might just judge others on how hard they work and…I may have a tendency to put work before relaxation, or heaven forbid, family and friends. Who had I become?

At the age of 32 (with 3 children and by now Company Director), I encountered a transformational moment. You know them when they appear – they interfere with your thinking, they agitate your mind. I had a leadership coach working with me, and I began to realise I had worked my way into a role that I could do well but did not love. With his help I began to explore who I was, why I had made the choices in my life so far, and importantly realised I had no real clarity on what I really wanted in life.

This transformational moment took me to where I am now, and I am very clear on who I am and my purpose in life.

I went back into education, and threw myself with passion into working out who I was, and learning all I could about how to help others find clarity, understand self, and to lead with both Head and Heart. The topic of my chapter is exactly that. How my self-discovery helped me 'find me', and to be brave enough to follow my passion for helping others find theirs. Leading with Head and Heart; with bold Clarity to achieve extraordinary results and fulfilled lives.

My first Aha! was to realise how much our childhood shapes our adult life. How our patterns and filters so deeply engraved from early childhood, shape how we make sense of this world and a realisation that people don't see the world as it is. They see the world as they are, through their own truly magnificent neural pathways primarily formed in the first two decades of their life.

Psychologist Maureen Gaffney, in her book 'Flourishing,' suggests there are three questions from childhood that can help us understand what drives our everyday patterns of behaviour and who we have become.

Question 1: As a child – what did you have to do to get your parents' attention?

I showed independence and initiative – that got their attention.

Question 2: What did you get rewarded or praised for?

I know I got praised for thinking for myself, using my initiative, working it out and getting on with it.

That has given me a very strong sense of independence and freedom, which is great as I'm never waiting for things to happen – I make them happen. The downside is I'm a very hard person to help and I seldom ask for help, even when I really need it. What do I often complain about? Why does no-one help me?

Question 3: What did you feel deprived of or feel you missed out on?

When I look back, I feel I was blessed with a very happy childhood, however if I was deprived of anything, it might have been advice and guidance. I don't remember my parents giving me any guidance on things like education, employment or other life choices. I believe this has been part of my life choice in the work that I do. I invest my life in helping others make better choices.

What comes to mind when you ask yourself these questions and how does that show up for you today?

Others in this book have written on the power of self-affirmation and self-belief, and we know we need to manage the judge and saboteurs that inhabit our mind, but I suggest before you can manage and control these, you need to be aware they are there. Then begin to understand how those limiting beliefs and judgemental patterns formed. Nothing is more transparent than how you lead yourself. 'Great Leadership starts within' so you'd better know who you are.

'When I discover who I am, I'll be free.' Ralph Ellison

Self-awareness combined with humility releases leadership that transforms people and their situations. Great leadership of you, your home, your family, your business, your life, requires extraordinary self-awareness, and willingness to continually learn and grow, letting go of what is within that will stunt your growth and impact as you lead others.

As a human being we are a connected system, everything is connected. Who we are leaks out, what we believe leaks out, our emotions leak out and our soul cries out. A pattern I have observed from my coaching clients is the link between our performance in business and what's going on in our personal life. As we encounter difficulties or success or happiness in our personal life, away from the work environment, our performance in work seems to correlate to the happiness/contentment we have elsewhere. In other words our performance matches our mood.

Of course, all leaders cast a Mood Shadow. Each of us creates our own systems – you, your family, your team, your business. They are all systems and as human beings we are on the alert, picking up messages from the system we are in to tell us if we are safe. Who you are on any given day or moment has impact on your own performance, and your team's performance. As a leader, your mood determines the mood for others around you. You are part of a system.

All systems are rigged towards self-preservation and we as human beings are 'meaning-making' machines. I make sense of the circumstances and happenings around me based on my neural pathways, my filters, my sense of the world. The older I get the more I realise the need to understand self, let alone others, is so valuable. Life is one long counselling session. We can discover new things that free us up, bring clarity, or help focus us to live a really purposeful fulfilled life. However, our system is wired to keep us safe.

Safety is an unconscious driver of behaviour. We are wired to protect ourselves, to keep safe. This goes back to thousands of years ago when we needed to be on the alert for danger; a sabre tooth tiger, or spear or arrow fired at us. It creates the fight or flight reaction. Today a lot of our fears are psychological, causing that stress response: fear of being rejected, being wrong, looking foolish, fear of losing status, or even fear of losing our job. We, as human beings, are still operating out of that same state, and 'fear loves a costume.' It will dress itself up as all kinds of excuses and valid reasons to remain safe, protect ourselves, not follow our dream, speak up, give feedback, or try something new. Psychologists suggest we are hard-wired to move towards safety 5 times more than purpose.

When you have too much fear in a system, you create fog. Fog in an organisation or relationship causes exactly the same response as experiencing fog when you are driving the car. You slow down, you hold tension in your body, you narrow your focus – you lack clarity. You withdraw. How that shows up in organisational behaviour is very evident. People don't speak up, don't challenge the status quo, don't give feedback or ask for clarity, for fear of the response, or fear of looking stupid. And of course, this delivers what I call 'groundhog day' results. You make progress, you see progress, even growth, but it slows down or worse, you relapse. The cycle leaves you frustrated and limits growth.

GROUND HOG DAY RESULTS

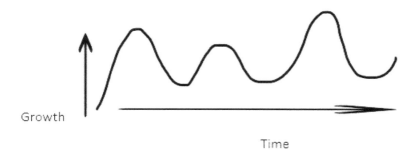

In order to move past this natural human desire to keep safe, we must create a clear compelling purpose. This requires courage, determination, and discipline; Head and Heart Leadership that drives us away from our fears, creating real Clarity and Purpose.

Much is written on the need for purpose, going right back to biblical times.

Proverbs 29:18 says, 'Where there is no vision, the people are unrestrained.' They can't focus, can't reach their goal, can't follow their dream. An older translation says, 'Without vision, the people perish.'

I've seen it many times – without vision, people lose the vitality that makes them feel alive.

The job of a leader is to help others find their sense of Purpose. People need to know how the work they do links to the organisational purpose and Vision – and they need Clarity.

Purpose enables passion, vision, energy, and without purpose, we feel lost and empty. We get stuck in the fog, drained of energy, or even passion for life.

I know to stay on the path to purpose needs grit and courage; the need to step away from staying within my known sense of comfort and safety. Leading with purpose requires great courage and bravery. Helping others find their purpose is your greatest challenge as a leader. It requires clarity, removing the fog, clear and relevant communication, an exquisite sense of self-awareness, and knowing when and if your Mood Shadow is pushing people back towards safety and mediocrity.

LEADING WITH VISION, PURPOSE AND CLARITY

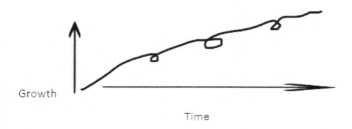

Here's the thing…There is no safe way to be great!

We are a Human Operating System – HOS. We are wired for both purpose and safety. Safety means we are protecting, allowing our fears to hold us back. When that happens fog enters the system, we slow down, become lesser versions of ourselves and in worst case, we freeze, stagnate, and results are mediocre.

Working with purpose requires courage, clarity, determination and discipline. The easy thing to do is stay in our comfort zone, and not face our fears.

So how do we help ourselves and others move towards PURPOSE?

We all have three basic human desires.

Belonging. We are hard-wired to belong. You only have to watch children at play to know how important it is to belong, that's why being part of a movement or tribe is so critical to us.

Valued. We are hard wired to feel that we have worth and are valued, not only in our own eyes, but in the eyes of others, especially those we care most about.

Love and be Loved. This is probably the strongest of human desires and a need we all carry. Trust, integrity, and loyalty are all a subset of love.

'People don't care about how much you know until they know how much you care.' – Theordore Roosevelt.

I can guarantee that if a relationship has broken down, whether that be a personal or business relationship, it will be because one or all three of these needs are being violated.

So, my journey to finding me, KNOWING WHO I AM, HAS GIVEN ME MY LIFE'S PURPOSE: To move people towards finding Clarity, Purpose: to lead with Head and Heart, with great self-awareness.

What lessons have I learnt that have helped me most? I've learned that too many times I've allowed my response to negatively impact the outcome. And that too many times I've argued to be right, when it was more important to be loving or kind. I've learnt how many of my old habits and patterns come from the sense of being left alone and the need to be independent, in control. As a young child, I took control, and it often shows up in situations when I don't need to be in control. 'I am a recovering controller.' Old habits die hard, but I have a choice, granted through great self-awareness.

'Between stimulus and response there is a space. In that space is our power to choose our response. In our response lies our growth and our freedom.' – Viktor Frankl

We may not be able to control the event, but we can control our response.

Event + Response = Outcome.

Our response depends on how we see the world – we see it through our own experience and upbringing. So…what is your response? Who are you? Do you provide clarity, removing fog that slows you and others down?

I encourage you to live a purposeful life, lead with Clarity and Purpose and make sure people you encounter know they belong, are valued and loved.

I have met many leaders in my over 30 years in business, and if there were a formula for becoming a great leader, I'd have had it bottled and probably be a woman of great wealth. However what I know above all, is that knowledge, information, and charisma might get you into a leadership role, but only character will keep you there.

CHARACTER

'Men of genius are admired, men of wealth are envied, men of power are feared; but only men of character are trusted.' - Arthur Friedman

A Great leader
Their Character is deeper
Ideas fresher,
Spirit softer,
Courage greater, **Leadership decisions** better,
Concerns wider, **Compassion** more genuine.
They **give away** power and **Ask great questions.**
They understand **the key role** of a leader is to **create other Leaders.**
**They strive for Clarity, leading from within with great self-awareness,
operating both Head and Heart Leadership.**

ABOUT THE AUTHOR

Kate is a highly sought after CEO, Coach, Mentor, Author, Facilitator and Speaker working globally with individuals and organisations. After a number of years in the corporate world, working her way up to Director level, she transitioned into the world of Leadership Development. She completed an MSc in Coaching, studied Neuroscience and worked to understand how we, the 'Human Operating System,' make sense of our world.

Kate founded Kate Marshall Ltd to offer a fresh approach to working with Executives, Boards and Leadership Teams both locally and globally. Her passion is 'People and Relationships,' whether in business or personal life, believing all relationships succeed or fail one conversation at a time. A recurring focus of her work is bringing greater clarity to every conversation and situation. By helping others become more self-aware, investigating perspectives and being curious about how situations and circumstances occur, they have access to better choices and better results.

Kate firmly believes the quality of our thinking determines the quality of our life. She is an advocate for both business and personal growth, challenging and encouraging others to make extraordinary choices. Her first book 'Agitate Your Thinking' was published in 2018. Her purpose is to make a positive difference to as many lives as possible. She is currently Chair of Cancer Fund for Children and past Chair of Women in Business.

Now more than ever organisations need to press the button for renewal. And innovation is the lifeblood of human progress. Teams are key to success here, as they act as catalysts of change.

DAGMAR BOETTGER

11

THE POWER OF TEAMS & VORSPRUNG DURCH TRUST & TEAMWORK

ENABLING THE POWER OF TEAMS TO INNOVATE

INTRODUCTION

'Thank you for your findings, your team defined an interesting growth market and yes, offers unconventional ideas, however ....' says the President of a corporate business unit while in meeting with high-ranking Committee members. 'What we see in your assumptions is still a big risk in the trend, so let us not fool ourselves, these ideas are risky and won't work! So, we better stop the project now, any comments?' There was no objection – the project was closed.

6 months of hard teamwork, across the globe, all units and corporate think tanks: GONE! Months of experimenting with different ideas, hypothesis and predicted scenarios: GONE! Our trust to be able to really contribute something meaningful in a CO2-reducing footprint project: GONE!

What happens every day in any large organisation happened to our global team[1] a few years ago. The team had been given the brief to; 1. develop 'out-of-the-box ideas,' 2. create solutions beyond given departmental and regional product lines, and 3. to challenge hierarchical thinking. The intrapreneurs in our team had pushed us far so we came up with portfolio additions, either cheaper versions for existing 'jobs to be done' or completely new solutions.

We had created out-of-the-corporate-box-ideas. How out-of-the-box-deciding was our top management? Had we misjudged our freedom and their trust? How could they not sense our good intention? Their inertia to look beyond existing 'boxes' made no sense, innovations emerge where new connections get woven. The company had lost in an even bigger way because our motivation to contribute was gone. Our trust in our power to realise ideas and ignite our entrepreneurial force was extinct. Others tried and succeeded. Coincidentally - years later – a Belgium start-up had turned 'our' ideas into fruition. The Innovator's Dilemma which Claydon Christensen describes had struck again?[2]

WHAT IS NEEDED NOW?

You might say: 'it is the job of top management to stop low potential projects.' True, yes. BUT: Can one or two high ranking executives cancel a project with the ideas of a dozen smart people, without giving them the grounds to test?

What is needed now, in between the 3rd and 4th industrial revolution, is to adapt to disruptive forces. Existing industries get disrupted by new business models, new market entrants from emerging markets and start-ups. With arising exponential technologies,[3] the speed of change will get even bigger and value chains broken apart – this is what revolution means. That is why entrepreneurial innovation power needs and is becoming a key driver of growth,[4] not just for tech-enabled businesses, but for any future-facing organisation.[5] While before 'knowledge workers' (Peter Drucker, 1969) managed knowledge to develop value by skilling a workforce to form productivity,[6] the 'smart enabling of human creativity' will replace this traditional management and give rise to a 'leadership of visionaries'. Ming Zeng, former ALIBABA strategist, Chief of Staff and INSEAD Professor, argues that whoever has a compelling vision of the future will attract players into their networks. The more connections the vision inspires, the more assets the visionary can mobilise. Jack Ma, Jeff Bezos, Steve Jobs, Alan Lafley, Richard Branson, Elon Musk, Ethon Brown all had a vision and look where it got them. Traditional leaders do not shape the future, they run machines.

Modern leaders drive innovation efficiency.

Unleashing creativity and building 'the co-creative potential (of teams) to ride the creative rollercoaster'[7] of innovation therefore becomes imperative. Team managers with diverse teams shape a new powerful and customer-serving drive to new growth. This is true in digitally transforming companies with 'cross-silo' teams, also in manufacturing companies as they move into industry 4.0 models, and it is true for agile teams. Innovation is a team sport.[8] Question is:

How can organisations build this powerful force in teams to turn ideas into something different of value?[9] What is the fabric of (team) leadership which enables their 'collective genius'?[10] How can organisations establish a culture in which 'behaviors driving innovation success come naturally'?[11]

Exchanging ideas within a group of people in trust can feel electric.[12]

In my work with teams[13] especially in China, I observed a powerful dynamic between three influences:

ENABLING INNOVATOR'S BEHAVIORS NEEDS LEADERS, TEAM MANAGERS AND MEMBERS ALIKE TO WORK WITHIN THE DYNAMIC TRIANGLE:

Innovative entrepreneurs and innovators share one DNA[14] with 5 behaviours and innovation teams show 5 traits: Curiosity, Customer Obsession, Collaboration, Adeptness in ambiguity and Empowerment[15]. Aspects of these can be trained, yet get easily blocked by lack of awareness, trust and psychological safety. Trust is the ultimate energiser for people. So enabling teams to trust themselves will help them feel confident to be innovative.

ENABLED CURIOSITY

Google hires curious people. Once, Google designed a billboard ad with a math puzzle. When answered correctly, the solution became an Internet address which lead the problem-solver to Google's recruitment page.[16] Today Google asks applicants to reflect first on their passionate interests. As they hire beyond skill, enduring passions, distinct experiences and perspectives make up for the future Googler.[17] Francesca Gino, award-winning researcher and professor at Harvard Business School, found out that to keep people curious is difficult. Whenever people start new jobs, she finds they report their curiosity decreases by more than 20% as they stop asking questions. Why? Francesca found out what blocks people: 70% feel their curiosity gets low as pressure to work rapidly, reluctance to take risk and fear of failure get in the way. So, if you want people to innovate invest in their curiosity. Andriano Olivetti, GM of Olivetti after 1938, encouraged all employees to stay curious. In 1960, workers had 2 hours for lunch: 1 for eating, 1 for 'eating' culture in a library or concerts. The investment paid off: in 1964, Olivetti introduced the first PC of the world.[18] A simple way to foster curiosity is to introduce new techniques to ask & answer questions. By using the 'Yes … And' principle of Improv theatre instead of a judgemental 'Yes … but,' team members will be encouraged to contribute and share perspectives. 'What if…' and 'How might we…' open conversations to new possibilities. Playfulness[19] also makes up for a powerful way: in my work with teams in China, playfulness made them try out, learn and giggle their way through experiments, thus shaping progress fast.

ENABLING CREATIVITY IN UNCERTAINTY AND AMBIGUITY

The creative process is full of 'Highs and Lows, thus shaping a creative rollercoaster.' It takes a mindset and practice to 'oscillate between the unknown and the known.' Dr. Nick Udall, CEO of Nowhere and founding member of WEF's global Agenda Council on New Models of Leadership, observes that creative teams move from 'creative tension' to 'creative realisation.' He clarifies how enabling creativity needs leaders to hold 'a safe container around those teams' and build 'voltage' for the ride. This 'not knowing' causes stress for leaders, especially those used to leading traditionally with linear prediction. But remember in exponential realities, enabling human creativity is key which requires leaders to manoeuvre the team through the rollercoaster. By intentionally disturbing existing ways of thinking, new creativity levels[20] will be sparked off. Balancing uncertainty with clarity on progress, building 'mental toughness' to cope with learning and failure (Janet Sernack, Founder & Head coach of ImagineNationTM, #1 Top Innovation Blogger) makes a new class of leaders and teams. According to Ed Catmull, co-founder of Pixar, trust thereby becomes the ultimate imperative for human creativity. Building trusting environments where people can 'solve problems to complex things, across the mess in the middle' means allowing for disagreements and abrasion without emotional impact. He observes an 'egoless state' when teams and leaders workout breakthrough solutions. Getting stuck is normal. Whenever that happens, teams call for 'Braintrust sessions'[21] where experienced storytelling experts of Pixar help discuss problems at hand. You say: we are not PIXAR, we are a traditional company, we cannot do this. Fully understood, 'don't throw any company's model' on top of your teams, try to initiate a shift and help teams speak up and share ideas. You might be surprised,[22] maybe it needs some work. The BEAN method of Innosight,[23] which hacks habits by establishing behaviour enablers, artifacts, nudges, and encourages new ways of working, is a good way to enable the shift. At Johnson & Johnson a 'kitchen' BEAN helps shape courageous conversations and creates space for ideas

ENABLE EMPOWERMENT

When BBC was challenged by cable TV in the early 2000s, the incoming CEO Greg Dyke initiated innovation by empowerment: he used his transition to ask 2 simple questions at all visits to major sites: 'What is one thing I should do to make things better for you?' and 'What is one thing I should do to make things better for our listeners and viewers?' The answers allowed him to form a compelling vision ('turn BBC into the most innovative and risk-taking place') and engage people eagerly: on Day 1, he gave out yellow penalty cards and asked employees to 'cut the crap and make things happen.' Whenever they saw good ideas being blocked they should raise those cards and unblock ideas. And they did. Within one year, BBC's audience satisfaction rose and ratings increased. Identifying blockers to empowered creativity is key because everybody's eyes and minds can contribute to solutions. Toyota asks employees to act as 'experts in their fields' and invites all to stop production by pulling the Andon Cord. Whenever they see a potential 'threat' to quality, they can stop and Kanban, a continuous improvement process drives innovative behaviours. When employees cannot see the full scope of a process or lack transparency, their confidence to take charge shrinks. That's why ALIBABA operates with one platform which is fully connected, synced and offers real time information transparency.[24] BASF introduced an 'Apple and Oranges' game to understand the tree to value creation in each unit and thereby help people see how and where they contributed. Innosight with its BEAN methodology helps too: at one company, employees designed the BEAN 'Shrink the HIPPO' to reduce the traditional shyness to take charge.

COLLABORATION ENABLED:

Building cross-functional teams is a first step to combine diverse expertise, perspective and skill. As members from different units connect to a common purpose, maximum 'co-creational potential' is grouped. That's where T or even π-shaped employees[25] might play a growing role as you surely want to employ the highest diversity in innovation teams. Having said that, it might be important to remember that 'the smartest person in the room, is the room itself.'[26] How do you build the glue in teams to act as one? If you ask people of their experiences in great teams, they always have a clear answer: there must be a balance on productivity and positivity dimensions.[27] Google's study on highly productive (and innovative Googler) teams found psychological safety to be the most crucial aspect.[28] Amy Edmondson, Novartis professor at Harvard Business School, defines the term as work environment where team members feel safe to take risk and be vulnerable in front of each other. To her, this safety builds dynamic collaboration, fosters tough feedback and difficult conversations. As former Google CEO Eric Schmidt says, Google is 'run on questions, not answers,' finding answers starts with allowing the flow of both - as input and a perspective, not truths. To enable co-creation, the rule should be that there is no right or wrong, but a flow of solution input. That's why whenever a project at PIXAR isn't working, the project is not judged by the project results, but the team's vitality. When 'engagement in the team is blocked and leaders are not listening' the project gets up for review. 'When you lose the CREW, that's a No-Go!'

MARKET-RESPONSE-ABILITY OR CUSTOMER OBSESSION

Innovation success depends how value-adding the innovative solution is to a user. When obsessed with customers and their needs, people develop a deep understanding of problems that matter, define 'the jobs to be done' and shape opportunities.[29] Empathising, visualising and typifying customers will help to 'design perfected and fortified experiences.' When GE Healthcare created the adventure MRI, designers observed how paediatric patients experienced scans with sedation and trauma. Empathising deeply, they turned children's fears into delight by reframing the scan into an exciting journey of pirates or astronauts: colourful designs and fancy invites make such a difference now. Innovations can also provide societal value: "care-calls" prior to visits of imprisoned relatives now reduce the emotional strain on relatives in Leicester prison. As they voice concerns and feel cared for, reduced stress allows getting used to a new family setting and helps to minimise the risk of family disconnect. When designing innovative user experiences, employees might be inclined by 'HIPPO[30]'- bias where teams subconsciously lean towards ideas favored by 'superiors'; Johannes Meyer, Design Thinking & Innovation Facilitator in Berlin, therefore puts all stakeholders in the design audience map, to clearly distinguish what senior stakeholders want and what customers need and want. Nick Skillicorn, Founder of Idea to Value, suggests to engage executives in ideation journeys. Participating stakeholders become sponsors to the process, especially when selecting which ideas to take forward. Their buy-in will positively boost test and experimentation (= known as IKEA Effect). In companies where bureaucracy is big, customer centricity programs refocus people's attention and drive a reset to re-exploring future market response: by asking teams to voice ideas on new customer service, a company-wide practice to re-design value becomes habitual to teams and change agility a growing pattern.

CONCLUSION

Now more than ever organisations need to press the button for renewal. And innovation is the lifeblood of human progress. Teams are key to success here, as they act as catalysts of change. Academic Research, innovation consultancies and my personal experience as coach for innovators suggest the same: teams and their leaders will make the difference in delivering innovations that matter to society, communities and companies. It's humans, not tech that will build new answers to (wicked) problems. Modern (top) leaders will have to lead with missions that matter. These missions will inspire people in existing operations to find new ways to improve and adapt how they serve people afresh. Far reaching missions will even invite people to contribute to totally unknown future opportunities. Innovation will still be hard and tough, but teams who ride the innovation journey and champion the messy bits with playfulness and a sense of humor, have a good chance to succeed. Finding support in their leadership's safe enablement and sound assertiveness will provide the glue and energy that matters during the ride. If our team had been supported by such a brave new leadership we would have won the startup game – and not the Belgian company - and our company would have gained a happy team and a CO_2 reducing product.

ENDNOTES

1   In order to keep things confidential, the author refrains from specifying the business case. The project aimed at developing ideas beyond existing business solutions to increase the sustainability-features of existing products. The team was therefore a cross-unit team, composed of regional, operational and sustainability representatives.

2   https://claytonchristensen.com/key-concepts/

3   See also http://podcast.diamandis.com

4   Read further www.mckinsey.com/featured-insights/innovation-and-growth

5   https://www.weforum.org/agenda/2015/09/why-innovation-is-the-key-that-will-unlock-global-growth/

6   It is information,' Drucker wrote, 'that enables knowledge workers to do their job.'

7   Dr. Nick Udall, 'Riding the Creative Rollercoaster', How leaders evoke creativity, productivity & innovation, 2015

8   https://www.mckinsey.com/business-functions/strategy-and-corporate-finance/our-insights/fielding-high-performing-innovation-teams

9   Innovation means 'turning ideas into something different that creates value'; read also 'Eat, Sleep, Innovate' by Scott Anthony, Paul Cobban, Nathalie Painchaud and Andy Parker

10   Linda Hill 'The Collective Genius: The Art And Practice Of Leading Innovation' By Linda A. Hill, Greg Brandeau, Emily Truelove, Kent Lineback

11   Definition of Innovation Culture, read 'Eat, Sleep, Innovate' by Scott Anthony, Paul Cobban, Nathalie Painchaud and Andy Parker, pp. 30ff
'Creative Confidence', Tom Kelley, David Kelley, 2013

12   'Creative Confidence', Tom Kelley, David Kelley, 2013

13   I worked with teams of multinational companies i.e. IKEA in China and Hong Kong between 2016-2020.

14   'The Innovator's DNA' by Jeffrey H. Dyer, Hal Gregersen, Clayton M. Christensen, A six-year study uncovered the origins of creative—and often disruptive—business strategies in particularly innovative companies: innovative entrepreneurs share five common discovery skills: Associating, Questioning, Observing, Experimenting, Networking, HBR, Dec 2009

15   'Eat, Sleep, Innovate' by Scott Anthony, Paul Cobban, Nathalie Painchaud and Andy Parker

16   https://www.businessinsider.com/what-google-can-teach-us-about-

solving-problems-2011-7?r=DE&IR=T

17 See https://careers.google.com/how-we-hire/

18 Francesca Gino, 'Rebel Talent, Why it pays to break the rules at work and life', 2018

19 In a review article, Li (2006) noted that playfulness contributes positively to the creativity of college students. Zhang (2011, Unpublished) developed a measure of playfulness for college students that consists of a seven-factor structure: namely, sense of humor, creativity, curiosity, activity, sociality, spontaneity, and pleasure. Taken from: An Initial Cross-Cultural Comparison of Adult Playfulness in Mainland China and German-Speaking Countries Dandang Pang; renE T. Proyer, 2018

20 Dr. Nick Udall, 'Riding the Creative Rollercoaster', How leaders evoke creativity, productivity & innovation, 2015

21 Ed Catmull, author of 'Creativity inc', helped establish 'Braintrust', a meeting format where teams ask for help from experienced colleagues and storytelling experts to shape new solutions.

22 One sponsor of a workshop in a Swedish retail corporation could not believe her eyes when she saw the creative results of her teams after 1 Day on Growth Mindset and Creativity in cross-silo-teams. People simply trusted themselves and became fast power creators.

23 'Eat, Sleep, Innovate' by Scott Anthony, Paul Cobban, Nathalie Painchaud and Andy Parker, 2020

24 Ming Zeng, „Smart Business What Alibaba's Success reveals about the Future of Strategy ', 2018

25 Together with partners, ADIDAS is creating the newest footware with innovative 4D Digital Light Synthesis. Carbon CEO and Co-Founder, Dr. Joseph DeSimone developed the process, called Digital Light Synthesis (DLS) which has the potential to bring customised high-performance products, like the new Futurecraft 4D running shoe, to any athlete. In her observation, some of the best ideas come from connections made between people who are new to the process and connections in communities that have never talked. https://www.gameplan-a.com/2017/04/meet-the-partner-behind-the-newest-adidas-shoe-futurecraft-4d/

26 'Eat, Sleep, Innovate' by Scott Anthony, Paul Cobban, Nathalie Painchaud and Andy Parker, 2020

27 'Teams Unleashed How to release the power of and human capital of work teams', Philipp Sandahl, Alexis Phillips, 2019

28   https://www.nytimes.com/2016/02/28/magazine/what-google-learned-from-its-quest-to-build-the-perfect-team.html

29   'Eat, Sleep, Innovate' by Scott Anthony, Paul Cobban, Nathalie Painchaud and Andy Parker, 2020

30   HIPPO means the 'highest paid person's opinion'

ABOUT THE AUTHOR

For the past 20 years, Dagmar has worked in Strategic HR Management and People Development with Global Multi-National Corporations and Small-Medium Enterprises, throughout Germany, France, Hong Kong and China. She specialises in Performance Management, Leadership Development and Change Management Projects.

Before starting her own consultancy, she developed the competency model for her employer and shaped change architectures for 5 regional change projects. With her deep understanding of APAC and European leaders and teams, her focus now is to support companies, particularly in Asia, to translate the effects of exponential change and tech-based disruption. By building company readiness and innovation competencies of teams and leaders throughout an organisation, new growth becomes possible.

She uses coaching and special innovation diagnostics to shift mindsets and strengthen cross-unit collaboration and leadership impact. She especially loves working with teams to see them unleash their innovation power and break organisational blockers to innovation. Her wish is for teams and leaders to make a difference through improving innovation everyday.

I am often asked, 'what's the most important thing we need to do to preserve our culture?' My short answer is, 'Uphold the values of the organisation.' My longer answer is about creating an environment where purpose is clear, and shared accountability is seen as a sacred duty to not let other people down when it comes to commitments, promises, and obligations.

12

JAN RUTHERFORD

FIVE TRAITS OF AN INDOMITABLE TEAM: LESSONS FROM EXECUTIVE EXPEDITIONS

GRIT

I was either cold, wet, tired or hungry a lot during my days in the army. On some days I was cold, wet, tired and hungry – all at the same time! It was those days when I learned a lot about myself, and when I learned about the people around me. It's easy to be calm, cool and collected when things are relatively comfortable, but when they're not, you start to see the character flaws – first in others, then in yourself. When I first entered the business world, it seemed that everyone was 'squared-away.' They looked good, spoke well, laughed easily, and they all seemed likeable. But it took a 'good' crisis, which only came around every few years to see what business people (as opposed to soldiers), were really made of. I often wished, 'If I could just get some of the business people out in the wilderness where they'd be a little cold, wet, tired and hungry, then we'd all see each other's true character – warts and all!'

When I started my business, I was determined to combine leadership development with nature to put my hypothesis to the test. Ever since, I've had the privilege of leading expeditions with Fortune 500 executives in the wilds of Patagonia, the Rocky Mountains, and on the glaciers of Alaska. We pair executives with military veterans who have served on some of the best teams the world has ever known. The executives participate in the Crucible® expeditions in order to take a step back, slow down, reflect, and reprioritise their professional and personal goals. At the same time, the executives possess a desire to help military veterans successfully transition to the business world.

One of my earliest memories as a soldier was learning how to lead a small patrol in the woods. While cold, wet, tired and hungry, we'd follow the person in front of us all while trying our best to be a good follower. At any moment, the instructors could call out your name as the new leader. If you weren't a good follower, then there was no way the team was going to help you be a successful leader. It was then I realised the collective will of the team is where the power is; the leader can't demand respect, can't will their way, or even outsmart the team. The leader has to first lead by showing respect to the team, and I have seen this proven over and over again in the military, in the business world, and on expeditions.

FIVE TRAITS

The successful and high performing teams I've worked with over the past four decades as a leader, team member, CEO, academician, consultant and expedition leader, all possess five indomitable traits:

1. Adventurous
2. Selfless
3. Driven
4. Dynamic
5. Protective

1. ADVENTUROUS – WILLING TO TAKE RISKS

When I think of indomitable teams, I think of those that are impossible to subdue or defeat – and the leaders of those teams are wired the same way.

Picture the towering sandstone towers and slot canyons of Utah in the Western United States; blue skies, hot days, cool nights, rugged terrain, and jaw-dropping sunrises and sunsets. During an expedition to this area, we had a woman on the team we'll call Mary. Mary was a very high-ranking executive with a large, multinational corporation. She was more comfortable in high heels than hiking boots, but she was out there fully committed to the experience, to hone her leadership edge.

It was the second day, and we needed to ascend a steep slope called a spur. It can be very steep on the sides of a spur, and the terrain in the Utah desert is rocky, sandy, and can be slippery. It was on one of these spurs Mary stopped our movement, and said, 'If I fall right here, I will die.' My instant thought was, 'You are not going to fall, and if you do, you will get hurt, but the probability of actual death is low.' Of course, I didn't say that. Mary caught her breath, and declared, 'I'm done. I am not going up there. Let's figure out an alternative.' I didn't argue with her, because one of our rules is that if you think something is unsafe, say something. And she sure did!

Before executing the alternative plan, I thought I would take advantage of a teachable moment. I said to Mary, 'I get it – this is really scary to you. And the risk is very visible. What about the times you ask people on your team to do things, and they're scared to death, but you think it's no big deal because the risk isn't apparent?' Mary looked down for a minute, and then said, 'You're right. I bet I ask people to leave their comfort zone all the time without any consideration, compassion, or flexibility.' I was amazed at how Mary's confidence allowed her to speak up and show some vulnerability. And like a self-perpetuating motion machine, her vulnerability seemed to give her even more confidence… to again show vulnerability and humility.

The lesson is that a high-performing team is willing to take risks. They're willing to attempt something, and not succeed. It only means failure if no lesson was learned. The balance is for a team to stretch themselves so they know how far they can go, but not stretch themselves too far they break. It can be a delicate balance, but when a team is willing and courageous enough to push themselves, they can learn their true capabilities. Nothing worth achieving is easy, and always requires an adventurous degree of discomfort, sacrifice, and self-discipline.

2.   SELFLESS – A SENSE OF DUTY

A moral obligation. A responsibility. A requirement to perform a task. That's how we define duty, and effective leaders make choices based on what they should do versus what they want to do. Selfless leaders feel dutybound to serve the greater good.

Wouldn't it be nice if all teams were comprised of near perfect humans? Engaged, committed, accountable, resourceful, resilient, humble, disciplined… But alas… we are all works in progress – often with unrealistic expectations of the people we select and lead.

Google's 'Project Aristotle' was aimed to figure out what makes for an effective team, and their findings boiled down to two simple things: an effective team has a safe environment where each person's voice gets equal time, and people display empathy towards one another. Simply – it's about being nice.

I had a boss and mentor once ask me whether my team, which was performing well, was truly committed, or merely compliant. With honest reflection, I realised it was the latter. So how do you know if your team is committed versus compliant?

During my time in the army, we had to carry a heavy backpack during long marches that involved taking turns carrying heavy objects (e.g., radios, machine guns, etc.).

When someone was engaged, committed, accountable, resourceful, resilient, humble, and disciplined, we'd often hear this:

'Let me carry that.'

An important point is that 'Let me carry that' could be a question, or a directive, and it can have a myriad of meanings:

> I want it now because I can see you're really struggling
> You look OK now, but save your energy – don't be too proud
> It's my turn, I haven't been doing my fair share
> I am trying to be a good team player, but I really hope you keep it longer
> Actually, I want to see you push yourself a bit further
> My turn to be the hero.

The other phrase that spoke volumes about an effective team was:

'Can you take this?'

It's not only great to share the load, but a selfless team with shared accountability and a true sense of commitment knows it's OK to ask each other for help. In fact, asking for help is an imperative, and a sign that the environment is safe to be vulnerable. Think about how great it is when someone you respect asks for your advice, or assistance. It shows you're trusted, and no team can function without trust.

As you reflect on what duty means to you and your organisation, ask yourself:

- Am I being selfless, and putting the needs of the organisation ahead of my own?
- When have I gone above and beyond for the good of the organisation?
- What would my colleagues predict I will grumble about most?

Henri Frédéric Amiel, a 19th Century Swiss philosopher wrote, 'Our duty is to be useful, not according to our desires but according to our powers.'.

3. DRIVEN – POSSESS HEROIC ASPIRATIONS

When hiring, astute managers use a job description as the roadmap for interview questions. They also know that no candidate will meet all the requirements, and the traits they're looking for fall into three categories: easy to train; moderate to train; and hard to train. The one trait I believe that is impossible to train – and that you must hire for – is a person who has an abundance of drive. To me, a collection of people with drive are the prerequisite for creating a team that has heroic aspirations beyond power and money – a collection of souls who truly want to make a difference in the lives of others.

But that drive has to be focused. I recall the story of a young army lieutenant, who was tasked with building a bridge across a stream for tanks. He desperately wanted to impress his soldiers as a leader of action – someone not afraid to get his hands dirty. He rolled up his sleeves, jumped in with a shovel, and started helping do the hard work. The lieutenant's boss appeared – a colonel. He motioned for the lieutenant to join him as he started walking from the bank of the stream to an overlook on a small hill. With cigar in hand, and without saying a word, the colonel motioned for the lieutenant to sit. A few minutes passed and the colonel didn't say a word. The silence made the lieutenant uncomfortable. After almost an hour, the lieutenant noticed he had not selected the best spot to build the bridge, and his soldiers were using a dated method for construction that could compromise safety. Upon noticing his blunder, the lieutenant said to the colonel, 'Sir, I… think…' The colonel abruptly interrupted him before he could say another word and said, 'Exactly!' The colonel got up and walked away.

The lieutenant was left with the dreaded task of informing the soldiers their work was for naught, and they'd have to move downstream, and start all over. It was then the lieutenant realised, his ego and pride ultimately created more work for his team. He knew the soldiers would rather have a smart and 'lazy' leader versus one who actually created more work. The lieutenant was driven, but placed his own needs above the heroic aspirations of the collective team.

A great team is driven – collectively and selflessly – to achieve heroic aspirations based on a common purpose. It's the drive to be extraordinary, not merely excellent; and it takes dynamic leadership focused on clearing obstacles and providing resources.

4. DYNAMIC – SLOW DOWN TO SPEED UP

It happens every time without fail. An expedition participant is selected to lead the team, which means setting direction and pace. Direction is pretty simple. Go from point A to point B, which usually means going up a mountain.

It only takes the first fifteen minutes of the expedition, and I will invariably tap the leader on the shoulder and motion for her to look back. The reaction is always the same.

'Geez – ugh. We're really spread out. I didn't think I was going that fast?' A few more moments go by, and as the leader reflects, she confesses: 'I do that at work, don't I?' I shrug to suggest she knows the answer, and she continues: 'Argh – but at work, I have no idea if we're all spread out, because I can't see effort, injury or easily determine who is the slowest person at any given time. OK – I will slow it way down, and check with the team more often to insure we all get there – together!'

No team is capable of going ninety miles per hour every day. Just like ascending a mountain, the leader has to read the team to, hear pains unexpressed, fears undisclosed, and complaints not spoken. The leader and the team have to sense when to step on the gas, when to ease up, and when to take a break. One of the world-class guides we use always reminds the participants that it's better to go slow than to take lots of breaks. My experience reflects his wisdom as well – more often than not, the team must **slow down to speed up.**

It also helps to create ground rules as a team before the work starts. Below is an example of the sort of ground rules we set before starting an expedition, which also sets character and judgement expectations:

- Initiative – If it needs to be done – do it
- If others aren't pitching in, talk about it
- Compliment the efforts of others
- Assume responsibility for learning
- Risk saying what you think
- If you don't understand, ask
- Enjoy the surroundings
- Maintain a sense of humor
- Help others learn and succeed

- Be kind and inclusive
- Push yourself
- Admit mistakes
- If it's not safe for the group – don't do it.

Pace-setting is vital, and the team has to know how to stretch each other to build confidence and daring to go the distance.

5. PROTECTIVE – A SAFE ENVIRONMENT

If you've ever had the privilege of seeing a herd of elk in the wilderness, you may have noticed they sit in a circle, and all face out. They are looking for predators, and they literally have each other's back!

Isn't that what we all want when we affiliate with other humans? Isn't that what makes for a great team? On expeditions, one of the ways strangers test the environment is through humor. It happens fast. Someone will tell a joke as a trial balloon to see if the team laughs. Over time, the group not only develops a 'group' dynamic, they also develop a 'humour' dynamic. That is, they start to risk saying what they think. And people don't usually joke with people they don't like or trust.

The Crucible® expeditions we run are designed to provide a powerful experience for executives, and transitioning military veterans. The goal is to foster the exchange of new ideas with regard to today's business challenges, and that's why selection is critical. We aim to take leadership abilities to new levels in an intense, dynamic and unpredictable environment with a focus on facing adversity with resiliency, resourcefulness, clear communication, and more effective decision-making. The secret?

> We select individuals whose character reflects what we value.
> We select for courage, humility and discipline respectively balanced with vigilance, confidence and creativity to produce a resourceful, collaborative, and focused team.

One advantage is the people come together as strangers with the knowledge that the team is temporary; we have a group of people with nothing to prove, protect or promote. In other words, no politics, no drama; a completely safe environment where people can speak their mind, take chances, experiment with humour, and practice holding their views lightly to hone their listening skills in a whole new way.

By slowing down and hearing the unheard we build focus. Being focused allows us to create an inspired common purpose – based on shared values and common virtues – that binds people together in an uncommon way.

CASE STUDY

Before we head out on an expedition, we use a behavioral analysis tool to assess soft-skills that are changeable, because we believe being a little cold, wet, tired and uncomfortable changes perspectives on resiliency.

What we've found is the military veterans are more motivated by commitment and obligation than flexibility and freedom. The confidence they display often has a steadying influence on others, but they can also come across as rigid and inflexible. After participating in the Crucible®, the veterans started to see the world - and their duty in it - through a different lens. Their drive for success and willingness to overcome obstacles and adapt changed significantly. And it persists. The veterans focus on their new work world with purpose and meaning along with a sense of duty.

After completing the expedition, many of the participants make significant changes and focus on pursuing work with more purpose and meaning.

BENEFITS

The benefits of a group of individuals focused more on teaming than individual leading are found in results, retention, and esprit de corps.

When teams are **adventurous,** they develop a tolerance for adversity and uncertainty.

Teams that are comprised with individuals who aspire to be **selfless**, seek feedback to learn from the experience and develop great self-awareness.

Those with vision and a bias to action, are **driven**, and constantly ask, 'For whose good do we serve?'

Dynamic teams are inclusive, constantly seeking the group's input, and they don't wait to ask for help when needed.

High-performing teams are highly **protective** – they stay calm and focused when it comes to judgment and decision-making.

IN SUM

I am often asked, 'what's the most important thing we need to do to preserve our culture?' My short answer is, 'Uphold the values of the organisation.' My longer answer is about creating an environment where purpose is clear, and shared accountability is seen as a sacred duty to not let other people down when it comes to commitments, promises, and obligations.

The military veterans' desire is always focused on continuing to serve. They often don't know how their skills will translate, but inherent in every fibre of their being is a devout sense of duty. They're driven by the desire to fulfill expectations and obligations with discipline and perseverance. This sense of duty is commonly thought of as taking care of the person to your right and left. Having someone's back. Not letting the team down. They shun those who criticize, condemn and complain. They know it's about being squared-away so they can focus on the needs of others rather than vice versa. The leader has to be self-reliant so as to be reliable.

As Bill George noted in his book, 'Authentic Leadership:'

> '... leadership emerged from their life stories. Consciously and subconsciously, they were constantly testing themselves through real-world experiences and reframing their life stories to understand who they were at their core.'

In the next chapter, Kanishka Misal shares how partnering powers an ecosystem to vastly improve collaboration, innovation, and overall performance.

ABOUT THE AUTHOR

Jan Rutherford entered the U.S. Army at age 17 (weighing 114 pounds), and spent six years in the U.S. Army Special Forces as a Green Beret medic and "A" team executive officer, as well as three years as a military intelligence officer.

Jan has over 25 years of business experience and has held executive roles in business development, marketing, sales, training, product management, and as a CEO. He is the founder of Self-Reliant Leadership®, leads Crucible® expeditions with executives and transitioning military veterans, and is the author of 'The Littlest Green Beret: On Self-Reliant Leadership.'

As a Senior Instructor at the University of Colorado Denver Business School, he teaches leadership in the U.S. and Ireland. He is also a LinkedIn Learning instructor. As a professional speaker, Jan was recognised as one of 'The Top 100 Leadership Speakers for 2018' in Inc., and is a TEDx speaker.

Jan also serves on numerous boards, and invests time helping military veterans transition to the business world. For the past five years, he has been the co-host of 'The Leadership Podcast.'

Jan is a dual U.S. and Irish citizen with a special affinity for Ireland and the wilderness of the Western United States.

The true potential of an ecosystem starts to come into effect when the individual entities begin to support one another.

13

KANISHKA MISAL

THE POWER OF WORKING AS AN ECOSYSTEM

LET'S START AT THE VERY BEGINNING

Competition: the activity or condition of striving to gain or win something by defeating or establishing superiority over others – Oxford Dictionaries

From an early age, we are taught to compete. We are hardwired to think of ways to defeat our opponents. It's ingrained into our DNA to strive for that spot on the winners' podium. And yet amidst the process of competing with one another, we often overlook what we could have achieved had we approached our challenges together, acknowledging and leveraging the human synergies at our disposal; synergies between our biological existence, the existence of other life forms, and the natural environment surrounding us. This way of thinking extends well into our professional career as we go on to lead teams, whereby we begin competing with other teams within our business. And soon, we are competing at scale with other businesses.

Don't get me wrong, I'm not against competition. But when we start to look at aspects of business through just one type of lens, we often fail to see the opportunities that sit before us had we been thinking differently.

THE FORMATION OF AN ECOSYSTEM

The Oxford English Dictionary defines 'ecosystem' as a biological community of interacting organisms and their physical environment.

Let us take a look at an example closer to our day-to-day lives to better appreciate the application of ecosystem led thinking applied to business: The good old taxi networks. For decades, every large or small city has had individual taxi operators, minicab service providers, private chauffeured rentals, etc. All functioning as independent entities trying to outperform one another. All fighting with one another to get a larger piece of the pie. Some went in for better cars. Others cut costs. The more creative ones managed to launch their own personalised mobile apps as the technology became mainstream and affordable. The challenge in their thinking was that they were all still working very hard to 'secretly' capture the other one's market share, operating in silos and pushing thresholds of efficiency at the cost of the driver - the most valuable member of the ecosystem – who was probably being paid the least from the margins being generated.

Until one day when a new operator looked at the entire ecosystem as one large interconnected jigsaw puzzle, with infinite possibility, zero physical boundaries and identified the <u>three central pieces</u> that combine to drive the millions of transactions - the passenger, the driver and the route. This operator orchestrated a simple, direct & digital connection between these 3 fundamental entities. The result was the formation of six new types of business evolving around - self-employed full-time drivers, part-time drivers (dads/moms/students supporting household incomes), vehicle financiers, technology providers (mobile/app/connection), service providers, legal & compliance agencies.

We have all witnessed the disruption this created in what was once believed to be an impenetrable marketplace. There is no question in my mind, some new players will further evolve this ecosystem for better or worse, however the fact that the status quo has now been challenged, opens up a pandoras box where only our thinking remains the constraint.

Another recent example has challenged the decades-old status quo maintained by large hotel chains in the hospitality sector as an aggregator of free space. This transformative business brought four key component parts into direct contact with one another without viewing them as competition - the guest, the host, the space & the destination. The result has been the creation of 24 divergent businesses (4x3x2x1). Some examples of the newer, innovative ones are - key management agents, digital home management devices, outsourced maintenance providers, room photography specialists, travel interior designers, daily rental agencies, local trip planners, meal deal providers, couch surfers, LGBTQ travellers, tax counsellors, etc.

Let us take a look at few more examples, where I will leave to your imagination the brands corresponding to the convergence of these basic entities:
1. The viewer, the content provider, the genre (comedy/horror/sports)
2. The job seeker, the employers, the job
3. The commentator, the content maker, the topic
4. The traveller, the airline, the destination
5. The foodie, the restaurant, the cuisine, the driver

A BUSINESS CONVERGENCE-DIVERGENCE OF ENTITIES™ (ABCDE™)

While there isn't a proven formula, one has normally observed there is a need for a minimum of 3 entities to converge in order to create 6+ diverging business entities (3! is mathematically = 3 x 2 x 1).

Similarly, when 4 entities begin to converge, at least 24 (4! is mathematically = 4 x 3 x 2 x 1) divergent businesses evolve.

The 3 basic converging entities are the:
1. Buyer
2. Seller
3. Product or Service or both

The 6 diverging business entities are often related to:
1. The traditional consumer
2. A breed of new consumers created through the model
3. Software infrastructure & maintenance
4. Hardware infrastructure business
5. Business support services for old and new types of services
6. Legal & compliance (often a litigation function to challenge the status quo)

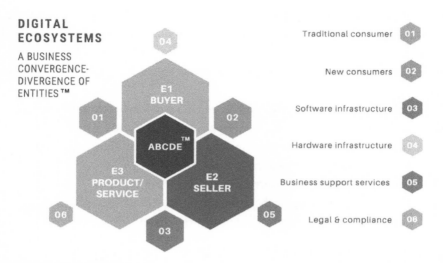

DIGITAL ECOSYSTEMS

A BUSINESS CONVERGENCE-DIVERGENCE OF ENTITIES™

04

E1 BUYER

01

02

ABCDE™

E3 PRODUCT/ SERVICE

E2 SELLER

06

05

03

Traditional consumer — 01

New consumers — 02

Software infrastructure — 03

Hardware infrastructure — 04

Business support services — 05

Legal & compliance — 06

THEIR INFINITE POTENTIAL

As the new ecosystems begin to co-exist and collaborate, they generate an even greater impact. Imagine the outcome of an overlap between a travel ecosystem and a food ecosystem. You could be having your favourite restaurant meal on a flight from London to New York delivered fresh to you at the boarding gate. Throw in the taxi ecosystem and that day isn't far when you could ride share your plane to a common destination.

THE BALANCING ACT & ESTABLISHMENT OF THE TRUE-NORMAL

When new ecosystems are formed, they also create the need for balancing performance & pay. The individual entities (driver or host or guest) try to outperform their own previous performance by offering better services or experiences for the value of the wealth being exchanged. But in doing so, they are increasingly likely to succumb to the performance pressures associated with behavioural evaluation, directly impacting every transaction. This is where ecosystems can begin to lose touch with the credibility and simplicity around which they were first formed.

TRUE-NORMAL. I have often defined this phrase as the era post-pandemic when the vast-scale adoption of technology, forced upon us in 2020-21, will begin to create & merge several new ecosystems. These ecosystems will tap into the traditional way of life while beginning to truly embrace & normalise the presence of digital in our day-to-day lives.

The true potential of an ecosystem starts to come into effect when the individual entities begin to support one another. There are many examples on social media surrounding the hospitality sector mentioned above, where an accommodation's host has redirected their guest to another host as a gesture of reciprocal goodwill, in exchange for alternative hosting dates, or a ride share app has been used to deliver food & essentials.

THE COMMON INFLUENCERS ENABLING SUCCESS

As organisations move towards the adoption of new business models, the degree of their success is driven by some common influencers widely observed across leading players.

1. **The adoption of digital technology** is probably the most significant one, leading to the highest degree of disruption between old and new operating models. Coupled with the presence of AI, AR, & VR in our day-to day lives, the consumer experience is, and will continue to soar to an unimaginable level.

2. **Managing consumers & partners over social channels:** we have all experienced to some extent the impact of real and fake feeds on social media and digital channels. Businesses with significant control on their digital presence are in a far better position to handle the social sentiment of their digital following, and perform any required damage control quickly and effectively limiting the impact such 'fake news' is able to create. However, while many of us may personally move to adopt, adapt or disengage with social networks, as businesses, we rarely have the same luxury of choice. If your consumer is spending over 12-hours consuming digital content at home, bound by Tier 69 restrictions, it stands to reason that you need to be present and serving them that content, or someone else will.

3. **Transparent transaction platforms** (in the near future leveraging block chain): Data is now the old-school physical currency – it's there, some of us use it, others have moved on to lighter, contactless payment methods. Transactional insights are the new 'cryptocurrencies' of the digital world. Understanding consumer behaviours, buying patterns and how they effect social sentiments and actions is just one of many examples of

the type of insights we are moving towards to drive business evolution. Ecosystems investing heavily in transparent transaction platforms, will have a leading edge over their more traditional competitors.

4. **The Undiscoverables™: T-he hidden talent in the ecosystem:** With the abundance of information, easy access to experts and quick re-directional support from social channels, talent is continuously developing both within and outside the organisation. Individuals are learning in new ways. There is a paradigm shift from classroom led human dependent learning into bite sized, user rates content consumption on the go. If anything, the recent pandemic has only proven, we can continue to learn if we have the will to do so. Unfortunately, traditional talent selection processes are still deeply embedded in several businesses. Their focus largely remains around measuring talent based on degrees, CVs, years of experience, references, etc. They are overlooking the significant change in the way people are learning & upgrading their skills.

AM I THE COMPETITION?

As one of the world's largest video content distributors explains, this phenomenon, with 70% of viewers binge watching content, 'sleep' has become their biggest competitor. Sleep minutes are the new trading currency with a tangible business value and quantifiable convertible $£€ rate. One of the most popular nano content apps in the world, with over 800mn users (500mn active), has a global average of 52 minutes per day per user. 1 extra minute on the app or a minute less of sleep, depending on whether you are the half glass full or half glass empty viewer, could translate into approx. £500Bn+ of ad revenue or approx. 1400 person years loss of productivity per day of the human species.

ABOUT THE AUTHOR

Kanishka is an accomplished business executive with close to 20 years of hands-on experience in cutting edge technologies, innovative business models & incubating new ventures. For much of this time, Kanishka has served with TATA Consultancy Services, in a wide range of leadership roles across industry sectors and technology domains. Having set up and operated businesses in India, US, UK, Europe, LATAM and Australia, he brings global insight into design thinking, product development and launch of platforms, services and solutions. His core areas of expertise are:

- Business architecture & strategy
- Managing large deals & partnerships
- Product design & development
- Talent Management as a Service

Kanishka is currently (2021) serving as the Chief Business Officer & CTO for the Route2Work Group. He is responsible for the group's strategy, business architecture & tech landscape, and has been a key founding member of the InfinityGlobal.IO team; an ed-tech and digital careers business launched in the UK in 2019, recently acquired by the Route2Work group.

Route2Work's goal is to level the playing field for undiscovered talent globally; connecting passionate people with meaningful education, training and career opportunities, via world-class technology. Our end-to-end digital solution for attracting, assessing, up-skilling & re-skilling talent has already proven to reduce an organisation's time to hire by >70%, and the cost to hire by over 45%. Commercial benefits are just the beginning. By turning our backs on traditional methods and leading our talent selection drives with technical skills assessments & behavioural diagnostics, R2W is uncovering the next generation of digital talent both inside and outside of an organisation. By upskilling or re-skilling, each individual can match their new role precisely, ensuring characteristic fitment within the role, their wider team, and the organisation as a whole. R2W has partnered with TATA Consultancy Services to bring to the UK their iON technology; one of the most powerful education technologies in the world, to make learning affordable, free in some cases, and accessible far beyond institutional boundaries. Their latest and most exciting venture is the launch of their digital market place, which connects people to opportunities and business to talent.

Purpose and belief have been key, the indicators and elements of a strong team have applied, 'we' language has been a focus, minimising interference has been critical, and the significance of truth and trust within the golden rules for accelerated excellence, have been relevant and clear.

TIM WIGHAM

14

MASTERING MOODSET TO SUSTAIN EXCELLENCE IN A CHANGING WORLD

In my final year at school I was the anchor for our house cross-country relay team. I was also ranked as one of the best runners at the school.

When I received the baton, I felt the overwhelming weight of responsibility to take the lead and finish strong, instead I mis-timed my charge to the front of the field and ultimately failed in my mission, I crawled across the finish line, then collapsed unconscious.

I woke up with a drip in each arm and the suggestion that I should not participate in the individual event the following week. My dream of winning the senior cross-country title looked set to remain just a dream. Thanks to the Sanitorium support, I rehydrated sufficiently for a return to sports in a few days, but was initially despondent about my chances in the individual event given my recent collapse.

I felt progressively stronger and more confident as it neared time for the individual run. My mood improved dramatically. On the day of the race I got the strategy spot on and found myself in front with 1 mile to go. It was then a case of hanging on to the lead, crossing the finish line, and enjoying the fulfilment of a dream.

When I look back at that small achievement from my school years, I realise it is a big reference point for how to overcome adversity, find the upside in a downturn, and simply help oneself believe that success can follow disappointment.

Fast forward ten years and I was a commando captain helping to restore peace in the West African country of Sierra Leone. A rebel army was advancing on Freetown, murdering and maiming hundreds of innocent civilians along the way.

My role was to fly onshore from the commando carrier, HMS Ocean, liaise with the spearhead battalion on the ground, and then lead my Mortar Troop of 60 marines as we adjusted a number of targets to ensure indirect fire capability when the rebels approached Freetown.

During that 6-week campaign in West Africa there were many threats and risks outside of our control. But what we could rely on was our training and our trust; trust in each other, trust in the system, and trust in the motivation of the marines on the ground. In other words, we focused on what we could control to lead a successful defence of the capital.

When I reflect on that situation, I realise how critical it was to sustain the right climate for the troops to deliver excellence in a dangerous place; to manage the mood, or moodset, for motivation and morale.

Mood is the background music, the ambiance, the feeling we have about an environment. Does it make us feel productive and energetic, or does it make us feel ignored and lethargic? In any team environment, one gets a sense of how people behave, how people are treated, and what is the state of morale. This all ties into the team mood, and this is fundamental to the acceleration of team performance from average to excellent.

People often ask me about the best initial indicators of a team performance culture based on first impression: I always answer that it is about the simple basics; good or bad, these indicators are typically representative of the overall performance picture.

The first indicator is whether members of the organisation are audibly bad-mouthing management or each other. It is amazing how prevalent this is, and therefore the absence of negative talk is notable.

The second indicator is whether meetings happen as advertised and on time. Unfortunately, many organisations struggle to start meetings on time and to keep meetings effective. Consistently punctual and valuable meetings are therefore significant.

The third indicator is whether people do what they say they'll do when they say they'll do it. All too often, incongruence is the norm: someone promises to get something done but then needs constant reminding. Early delivery on small promises is a massive positive.

Performance culture has much more complexity, but these initial indicators have served me well for many years.

Here are some of the subtle behavioural indicators of a true team in any setting, of a team much more likely to achieve a high-performance culture, based on my observations and experience.

The first element is basic courtesy. This is such a fundamental one. It manifests in various daily interfaces, such as greeting colleagues when you see them and responding to communications in a timely fashion. It needs to be a two-way street; if it feels like one party is constantly having to initiate the courtesy, there is no true team.

The second element is basic trust. This builds on courtesy. A true team has formed and stormed to the extent that trust has been earned. It allows for personal growth and for individual expression to benefit the collective. If concerns about trust are regularly voiced, or micromanagement is in evidence, there is no true team.

The third element is basic empathy. This builds on courtesy and trust. It means that team members are interested in the challenges of colleagues and that they seek to understand different points of view. If there is no sense that team mates genuinely care or can step into the shoes of others, there is no true team.

The fourth element is basic energy. This is an essential ingredient in any successful team. Energy can be seen and sensed, as can lethargy—an opposite element synonymous with poor performance and disjointed teams. If there is a lack of energy, there is no true team, or at least not one that is likely to achieve high performance!

Bringing it all together; in my experience, true teams consist of courteous individuals with high levels of trust, genuine empathy, and high energy. These elements can be detected in a relatively short space of time. Deficiencies in any of these areas will detract from team togetherness and prevent high performance. Get the basic elements in place and build a true team.

The language that we use as leaders also influences the team dynamic and human behaviour; workers and followers conform to the subtle cues of their management. Our words play a major role in team health and team well-being.

Two words that can have a disproportionately negative impact on morale and performance are *I* and *they*. Thankfully, a word that can undo that damage, if adopted as a better replacement, is *we*.

All too often, I have experienced the disappointment of hearing 'I will decide' when it should be a team decision, or 'they messed up' when in fact we were all involved somehow.

Incredibly, very little is lost, but a huge amount is gained if instead the message is, 'We messed up, and we will decide how to improve together.'

I have been on so many projects where the ubiquitous 'they' are to blame that I wonder whether '*they*' have ever done anything right!

How about a switch to a world where the only time we use *I* or *they* is to say, 'I made a mistake,' or, 'They did an excellent job.' Otherwise, use *we* to include team and togetherness.

Based on the *we*-cultures I've been privileged to serve; you'll be amazed at the positive impact on morale and performance that this subtle shift can have.

Sir John Whitmore, author of the book *Coaching for Performance*, references a superb formula, P = p - i (Performance equals potential minus interference). I love the word *interference* in this context because it perfectly describes many of the real and imagined obstacles that we allow to detract from our own, and our teams' true potential.

Bruce Tuckman devised the forming – storming – norming – performing - adjourning model for team progress. Natural progress to performance can be accelerated with deliberate effort. The difference between the two curves is 'tolerated interference.'

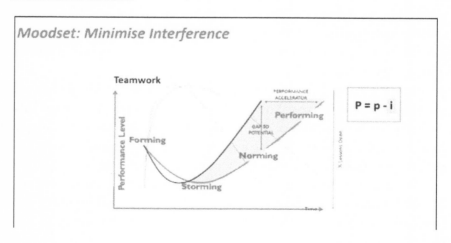

If we can remove this interference, we can certainly enhance moodset, our own and others. Interference that I have encountered with frontline teams includes unnecessary meetings, irritating micromanagement, and overwhelming bureaucracy, as well as, nowadays, unlimited social media. Ask anyone affected by these issues about their mood, and you can expect them to give a less than positive response.

Netflix recently released a fascinating series called *The Playbook*. I watched every episode in one go. It was like intravenous inspiration for me. The insights from Jose Mourinho and Patrick Mouratoglou were especially intriguing because their guidance influenced some of the most talented and egotistical athletes on the planet. All five of the episodes provided principles for performance from proven practitioners. I was then able to analyse these phenomenal pointers and identify trends while also reflecting on my own playbook for 'moodset' mastery.

Some say that a corporate team is different to a rig team, which is different from a sports team. A factory floor is different to a shop floor, which is different from a football pitch or a tennis court. But there is a common denominator – people. And to get the best out of people is a craft which requires relentless curiosity and infinite service.

I am an avid reader, drawn to authors like Simon Sinek, Malcolm Gladwell, and Matthew Syed. These authors are some of the most respected voices when it comes to what it takes to unlock 'Great'. I learn from them and many others. Their findings often reveal further fascinating ideas about how sustainable progress has been made, and what we can learn from societies, communities, and outliers.

Mastering moodset is particularly important at this present time when many are working in isolation. As with locker-room inspiration for athletic excellence, the subtle cues for optimal productivity wherever we work, are worthy of deliberate focus in order to achieve measurable progress, and of course in order to celebrate every small success!

I analysed the Netflix series for consistency and created a top five informed by the list of 27 ideas. I got to this set of guidelines; five golden rules for accelerated excellence.
1. Start with the Truth.
2. Always be the Underdog.
3. Seize our Opportunities.
4. Together as a Trusting Team.
5. Forward to the Finish.

The best quote of the series for me was this one from Patrick Mouratoglou who coaches tennis superstars like Serena Williams...

'Your body language is telling me everything I need to know.' Body language truly is the language of our moodset.

In his book, *The Infinite Game*, Simon Sinek's chapter on Trusting Teams should be required reading for literally every leader in every workplace in my view. He uses excellent examples to make exceptional points. One of my favourites is his reference to the US Navy Seals.

The Navy Seals have a great measure to determine the kind of person who belongs in the Seals. Performance on the vertical axis, versus trust on the horizontal. Performance is about technical competence; trust is about character. One Seal apparently described it thus: 'I may trust you with my life, but do I trust you with my money or my wife?' It is the distinction between battle-physical safety and overall-psychological safety. One of the highest performing organisations on the planet prefers individuals in the bottom right quartile than in the top left, because the latter are typically narcissistic and toxic. The Seals select for character first. Trust helps build an elite team, whereas high performing individuals, only looking out for themselves, endanger a team.

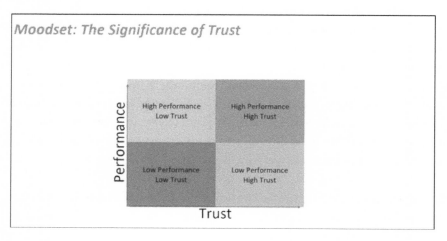

Sinek notes that culture equals values plus behaviour, these are the metrics for trust and performance. How people feel affects how they do their work. Strong cultures have safety in relationships - and in the next chapter, Chris Paton will explore how that safety is created and maintained. High performing teams start with trust, but this moodset needs to endure over time and that takes awareness and focus.

As a father of three young children, working from home due to the COVID-19 pandemic in 2020, while my wife home-schooled the kids and we strove to create the conditions for harmony, I've probably learned more about community-moodset than ever before. But the points made above were reinforced: Purpose and belief have been key, the indicators and elements of a strong team have applied, 'we' language has been a focus, minimising interference has been critical, and the significance of truth and trust within the golden rules for accelerated excellence, have been relevant and clear.

Sustaining excellence in the face of constant challenge and change is a truly fascinating pursuit. It can be done if we understand how to enable the right moodset in each setting.

ABOUT THE AUTHOR

Tim Wigham grew up in Southern Africa and has dual British and South African citizenship; he served in the British Commandos for eight years between 1992 and 2000.

After completing his MBA in Cape Town in 2001, Tim specialised in the facilitation of executive leadership breakaways across a range of industries to build strong cohesion, as well as clear strategy, mission, vision, and authentic company values. In the sports industry, Tim has worked on mental toughness with several of the Springbok Rugby players who went on to be World Cup winners in 2007.

In 2008, Tim began coaching leaders in the offshore energy sector. He helped to develop and evolve a method which improves team performance in high-cost, high-risk environments, through the implementation of belonging cues and improvement disciplines. As a frontline coach, Tim has worked in Africa, the Middle East, Asia, and Europe.

Tim is now a Director at Exceed Energy in Aberdeen, Scotland. Since 2012, he has trained and led dozens of performance coaches, who in turn have helped clients to save over half a billion dollars, by accelerating the team learning curve and implementing efficiency savings during long campaigns.

Tim has authored four books. He also coaches executives and leaders who are looking to remove interference and unlock their potential.

He is married with three young children; his main interests include writing, reading, travel, and competitive CrossFit. He also enjoys blogging about inspiration on his author website www.inspired-books.com

This sense of belonging, or inclusion, is one of the 4 stages of 'psychological safety' alongside, safe to learn, safe to contribute, and safe to challenge the status quo. So, in order to reach the point where people are comfortable to challenge existing thinking, they first need to feel part of the team. They need to believe that mistakes are allowed, provided we learn, and that it is good to put their thoughts forward.

CHRIS PATON

15 A SAFE SPACE TO TALK - THE IMPORTANCE OF DIVERSE THINKING

The rhythmic thudding of the rotor blades lulled me into fitful sleep as I sat in the back of a hot, noisy Chinook helicopter flying into Afghanistan's Helmand Province in September 2008.

The military aim in Helmand at that time was to create a protected 'bubble', which contained a safe zone for the Afghan Government and overseas aid agencies' staff to work in. Our predecessors had done a great job of fighting to establish this safe space and had set up a series of bases that acted as an outer defensive barrier to protect it.

In the 12 months leading up to our deployment, all our preparations and planning revolved around the premise of holding this protective barrier, improving the stability of the safe space and building on the success of our predecessors. We believed that we knew exactly what we needed to do and had considered what might go wrong, including attacks on one of the outer bases.

My own base, which housed the headquarters, sat in the very centre of the protected zone and it was to here that the Chinook touched down, jolting me awake and giving me my first sense of the Helmand heat.

But, on the fourth day of the tour, even before the rest of my force was fully in place, my base was attacked by 400 insurgents that had bypassed the outer bases. They began shelling us with rockets and mortars whilst launching a coordinated ground attack. We fought back with our own ground troops, helicopters, Afghan Army colleagues and Police. Throughout the course of a long, tense and volatile night, things ebbed and flowed but ultimately, we prevailed.

When we started to analyse what had happened – the key question was: how did we miss the fact the 'safe zone' was so vulnerable? Why had we perhaps taken for granted the security barrier provided by the outer bases?

My Helmand province experience sits in what Pullen and Donald[1] call the 'unknown knowns'. These are described as problems/concerns that people within the organisation are aware of, but haven't communicated, either through fear of challenging the hierarchy, or through ambivalence ('what's the point, no-one will listen'). These unknown issues are a catastrophe, which in hindsight, could have been predicted, but either through organisational culture, governance or casting a blind eye, they simply do not come to light until it is too late.

This was exactly what happened to us. There were individuals, who had become aware that the outer bases were not a solid barrier. There were also people who were concerned that the focus of combat power on the outer bases left a dangerous vacuum in the central 'safe space', but their voices were not heard.

So why did these 'unknown knowns' not come to light? Why was it that something well understood at the granular, tactical level, did not percolate up to the leaders who needed that information the most?

I don't think we will ever know exactly why, but my personal belief is that it had a lot to do with the people who had the information feeling like they didn't have the 'right' to express it, or felt it wasn't safe to do so without retribution/sanction.

As my story seeks to illustrate, helpful disagreement is a good thing. While helpful disagreement is the outward expression, or 'challenge' to the leadership, it relies on diversity of thinking as the igniting spark. The question on your lips is likely to be 'how do we create the space for that to happen'?

BUILDING TEAM SAFETY

There are a number of factors which drive psychological safety, but the one needed above all others, is a sense of 'belonging'. As social creatures we are programmed to respond to all sorts of verbal, non-verbal and environmental triggers. We are also acutely aware of the need to 'fit in' with new groups – we just can't help it. We respond to patterns of behaviour and language in our family, workplaces and social groups, and subconsciously (and consciously) match it as swiftly as we can.

This presents a problem when we want to create a safe space for constructive dissent and debate. It runs contrary to millenia of evolution and social structures. It feels wrong to buck the trend of the group; to step out of line; to offer what may be perceived to be an unwelcome comment or challenge.

In fact, according to Timothy R. Clark[2], the opposite is true. The stronger the bond among the group, the more likely people are to offer a genuine opinion without pretence. Well-developed, cohesive groups are settled and feel safer – so the opportunity for honesty increases.

This sense of belonging, or inclusion, is one of the 4 stages of 'psychological safety' alongside, safe to learn, safe to contribute, and safe to challenge the status quo. So, in order to reach the point where people are comfortable to challenge existing thinking, they first need to feel part of the team. They need to believe that mistakes are allowed, provided we learn, and that it is good to put their thoughts forward.

To that end, it is wise not to have a debate with a very mixed group of people who have only just met one another. Work hard to develop relationships between those individuals ahead of time, set them up as named teams and get them working together on low-level issues, to share insights and solve tasks before you broach more challenging debates.

THE CHALLENGE OF DIVERSE THINKING

Having seen a number of very close-knit teams in action, both in the military and commercial spheres, I would think there is a 5th stage to Timothy Clark's model – one beyond challenging the status quo; which I would call 'the comfort zone'.

Building an incredibly tight and cohesive team in which people are happy to challenge one another is clearly a good thing. But this team, if left unchanged for a long period of time, can become too comfortable with each other and start to settle back into a comfort zone. They know each other so well that there is no need to challenge, as they can predict what others will say. They ease into a rhythm which feels familiar and comfortable, trending back to not wanting to rock the boat. This can often lead to Group Think and a drop off in performance, as suggested in the illustration below.

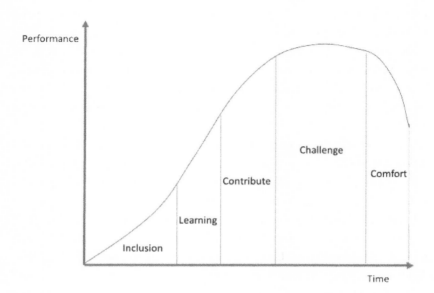

What we really need is diversity of thinking – which implies either (a) new people joining the group, or (b) bringing people into the debate who aren't part of the existing group, and who rarely work in direct and close links with each other.

Bringing new people into the group is something most of us recognise as being a good thing. New people bring fresh ideas, fresh thinking, and fresh approaches. But it can, if not carefully handled, damage that core sense of group safety. With new people joining it, the team needs to feel a clear sense of safety through inclusion, learning and contribution. So there is a fine balance as to how much fresh input can be absorbed by the system at any one point in time, little by little seems to be the best approach.

But this doesn't answer the question of how to create a safe space for a really diverse group of people who will bring a lot to the table, with significantly different frames of perspective, but who, by default, are not a coherent group. So how do we do that?

USING GAMES

We are all familiar with being 'out of our comfort zone'. We are perhaps less familiar with the way in which it can be used to create a safe space. If an individual, or a number of different individuals, are brought into the 'home turf' of an existing group, they feel uncomfortable. In contrast, the home team feel secure and even slightly superior.

But if we get everyone into an unfamiliar setting, it evens things up. There are a few ways to do this, such as taking everyone to a different physical location which they are unfamiliar with – the classic business 'offsite'. It is often mocked as a cliché, but it works.

The other way to create a level playing field is to put people into an unfamiliar context, such as a game. Gamification has become quite a growth industry for this very reason. It doesn't require the rental of an expensive offsite venue, just to put people into an immersive experience, which is new to all of them.

If we think about it, this makes sense. Games are seen as childish by some….. but children are invariably honest, open, share their fears and like having fun, without filters - so what better example could we have?

Even as adults we all understand the principles of a game – that it should have rules, be fun, challenging, engaging and have definite outcomes. If we apply this to commercial or even personal situations then, for a specifically defined period of time, creativity and challenge is allowed to flourish. It also creates an environment where failure is allowed to happen.

There are a huge number of gaming methods out there; Red Teaming, Wargaming, Thinking Hats, Pre-Mortems, Devils Advocate, the list goes on. These take a bit of time to learn and to apply effectively. My suggestion is to avoid books that tell you gaming is all about competitive intelligence and playing you versus your competitor. Yes, competitors are a part of what might cause a plan to fail, but so are a host of other factors; over selling, poor quality, market changes, regulatory changes, or an ambivalent workforce.

Facilitation is also key. If you are going to convince a group of people to take part, you only get one shot. The game needs to be well-run, coordinated and managed. You need to draw out learnings and capture those, or the session is simply a fun way to challenge thinking, without any actions to correct identified weaknesses.

Building stronger teams, encouraging learning, growth mindsets, and using games as a vehicle for positive challenge are all useful outcomes, but they essentially boil down to the same thing: 'helpful disagreement'. If we treat people in the right way, and are ourselves treated well, it gives us the confidence to ask 'does this make sense' and to call out when we feel things are heading down the wrong tack. This requires leaders to be open to questions and critique – to be vulnerable – which, in turn, creates a culture where individuals feel empowered, and so momentum builds, particularly if contributions are recognised publicly as having been valuable.

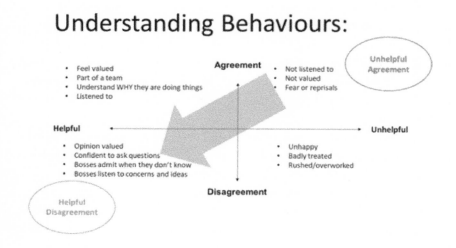

Understanding Behaviours:

It may sound odd, but there is such a thing as 'unhelpful agreement'. This is when people in the team don't raise objections to a course of action. This lack of objection is seen as 'consent' and the organisation ploughs on. There are many reasons why people are reluctant to put their point of view forward, sometimes it is due to a sense of never being listened to, not being valued, or for fear of reprisals.

Other times, it can be as simple as 'not wanting to upset others', as characterised by the **Abilene Paradox** – defined by Jerry Harvey in 1974 from an experience he was privy to:

On a hot afternoon, a man and his wife were visiting his in-laws in Coleman, Texas. Although they were comfortably playing dominoes on a porch, the father-in-law suggests that they take a 50-mile trip to a place called Abilene for dinner. The man's wife says, 'Sounds like a great idea.' The husband, despite having reservations because the drive is long and hot, thinks that his preferences must be out-of-step with the group and says, 'Sounds good to me. I just hope your mother wants to go.' The mother-in-law then says, 'Of course I want to go. I haven't been to Abilene in a long time.'

The drive is hot, dusty, and long. When they arrive at the cafeteria, the food is as bad as the drive. They arrive back home four hours later, exhausted.

As they discuss the trip, they come to the realisation that none of them had actually wanted to go. The initial suggestion was only made because the father-in-law thought people were bored and the others went along as each agreed, so as to not be out of step with the group.

This type of collective harmonisation is common. As mentioned previously, we have evolved over thousands of years to be part of a group. In mankind's early history, to be outside of a group generally meant being eaten by a wild animal, so we are hard-wired to conform and fit the mould.

I am firm believer that diversity of thinking is crucial to the successful outcome of any plan. Essential reading on this subject is Matthew Syed's excellent book 'Rebel Ideas'. Without diversity of thought and contribution, we inevitably fall into the trap of doing what we have always done and, by default, getting the outcomes we have always had.

That is the trap we fell into in Helmand in 2008 and is what led to me becoming somewhat of a zealot on the need for all organisations to create the safe space within which, challenge and a degree of dissent can flourish. Not to the point of organisational breakdown, but definitely to a level at which everyone feels a bit uncomfortable. It is at the boundary between discomfort and breakdown that true innovation and creativity exist – and the area where risks can be identified.

Much of this rests on the importance of an organisation's values and genuinely understanding them, believing in them and living them on a daily basis, which Bob Keiller will expand on in the next chapter.

Ultimately, feeling safe to express your views is something that applies across all aspects of our lives and relationships. It's an important part of being who we are and how we build strong bonds with those around us. I know that I have stronger relationships with people who tell me when I'm heading on the wrong track. It's all about balance – if those same people tell me when I'm doing something well, I'm much more prepared to listen and absorb the critique when it comes. It's not something I find easy, I don't enjoy learning I'm getting something wrong, but I am always learning, and growing, as a result.

ENDNOTES

1   Bolt from the Blue: Navigating the world of corporate crises by Mike Pullen and John Brodie Donald.

2   The Four stages of psychological safety – Timothy R. Clark

ABOUT THE AUTHOR

Chris is the Managing Director of Quirk Solutions, a consultancy specialising in the human factors behind change, transformation and risk.

At his core, Chris has a deep sense of service, and a determination to help whoever he can, however he can and whenever he can. Some of this comes from his previous career of 18 years in the military; much of it though is 'just who he is.' He values family, friends, fun and reflection – though time for reflection is often in short supply.

After many years leading people in combat and peacetime, he came to the conclusion that he is the best version of himself when he is not at the forefront….but being the invisible support to others, enabling them to achieve their goals. When he was leaving the military, he sought a career that would allow him to do this and consultancy was the route he chose. Helping client companies to perform well means their people are happier and lead more stable lives, which allows Chris to perform the role he does best; guiding and encouraging, not directing.

He is a recognised leader in the field of gaming, transformation & change and has delivered consultancy to a wide range of public and private sector organisations. He has lectured at the London Business School Executive Education programme, and has delivered keynote speeches in New York, Berlin, London, Glasgow, Manchester and Cannes. Published in the Harvard Business Review in 2010 with an article on managing complex and uncertain situations, Chris has also had an article in Strategy Magazine in 2018, and Business Continuity Magazine.

In his former career, Chris was a Lieutenant Colonel in the Royal Marines and advisor to the Cabinet and National Security Council on the Afghan strategy. He saw active service in a wide range of places including Northern Ireland, Kosovo, Georgia and Afghanistan. His most senior role saw him as Head of Afghan Strategy to the David Cameron Government, where he was responsible for overseeing the strategy to extract all UK combat troops and their equipment in a 2-year timeframe. This was one of the largest strategic initiatives the UK had undertaken for over 60 years.

Chris melds his government-level experience with a decade of consultancy in the commercial sphere, supporting clients such as Lloyd's Corporation,

Waitrose, Shell, Unilever, Linklaters, Mercedes and the UK National Health Service. His approach is to ensure that all perspectives are brought to the table with 'diversity of thought.' He takes great enjoyment from helping teams generate new insights that hadn't previously been considered, by enabling everyone to offer their thoughts in a safe space.

A fluent French speaker with a Masters Degree in International Liaison and Communication, Chris is a Fellow of the Strategic Planning Society as well as a Fellow of the Society of Leadership Fellows, St George's House. He is a proud father and husband, and someone who tries to correct his many faults as best he can - but recognises that is an ongoing project!

If people don't feel that the values are genuine and being practiced and applied across the organisation, they won't see any point in committing to them.

And if they don't understand the values, it's difficult to see how they can believe in them.

And they cannot understand the values if they don't know they exist.

16

BOB KEILLER CBE
DOING CORE VALUES

In 1993 I was working as a supervisor on an offshore platform in the middle of the North Sea. I worked offshore for two weeks at a time and my boss was the Offshore Installation Manager – known as the 'OIM'. My boss was called Alistair.

One evening, Alistair asked me and another colleague, John, to come into his office.

'I want to give you both some feedback.'

He paused. Then he looked directly at us and told us:

'You are shite, and you will be shite 'till I say you are not.'

He paused again – maybe he was going to give us some detail, maybe explain what he had observed and give us some coaching on how to improve our performance. But no.

'Okay that's it, on your way!'

I was stunned. Feedback is supposed to be helpful; it is supposed to be useful and it is supposed to be balanced. This was none of these.

But it wasn't unusual, I had seen many examples of clumsy managers treating people poorly and failing to get any meaningful response from them. This strengthened my conclusion that there had to be a better way.

Years later, I found that building an organisational culture based on Core Values that define acceptable behaviours, makes all the difference. I also came to understand what a positive lasting impression it can leave on people. Former employee, Scott Saunders, posted a comment on LinkedIn on the 6th of July 2020:

PSN really was a great place to work. You couldn't have met more engaged, more enthusiastic and friendly people. I left in 2010 and still miss the buzz around the place. I don't think I appreciated it enough when I was there, it's only looking back you realise how great the people were from Bob Keiller at the top, right down to each new intake of graduates.

Now, I am assuming that you are already convinced that having really effective Core Values in an organisation is a good idea – otherwise you are not going to be interested in a chapter about 'Doing Core Values'.

So, I am not going to talk about the benefits of having a great culture built on sound values.

I am also assuming that you already have your values defined and written down. How to do this is the subject of another discussion.

I want to talk about the challenge of taking a well-crafted set of organisational core values and bringing them to life.

You'll be glad to know, that embedding Core Values is relatively simple. Not easy, but simple. It's all about getting buy-in, from your team. I found that there were four elements to this:

1. Get people to know and like the values
2. Get people to understand the values
3. Get people to believe the values
4. Get people to use and live the values

If people don't feel that the values are genuine and being practiced and applied across the organisation, they won't see any point in committing to them.

And if they don't understand the values, it's difficult to see how they can believe in them.

And they cannot understand the values if they don't know they exist.

STEP ONE: AWARENESS

Building awareness of Core Values is straightforward. Here, the point is simply to introduce and explain the Core Values, making people aware that they exist and that they will now inform all company processes and decisions for the good of the organisation and its people.

This entails all the basics you would expect - announce the values, communicate and market them, disseminate information, essentially get the message out there. It can be as simple as a memo or as elaborate as an experiential event. Whatever you do, you need to do it repetitively and often. Don't stop at one email, bombard them! Send postcards, have Values inductions, make booklets, shoot videos. Do whatever you have to do to get the Core Values out there.

One of the things I did with my staff was to have each of them sign for a copy of a book with the Core Values in it. I asked for signatures because I wanted people to make a psychological connection to having read and understood the values, and what we were working to achieve. The idea was that once they had signed and acknowledged receiving the book, there was no excuse for not knowing and understanding, and in time, buying into, the Values.

Of course, I expected that the vast majority of people would sign for the book and put it in their desk, or in their boiler suit pocket and forget about it. I didn't for one-minute think that was the end of the conversation, so I kept communicating the values, and making sure there was as much awareness of them as possible in the company.

STEP TWO: UNDERSTANDING

You can tell a ballerina how to do a jete. You can even show her pictures, or video, or live demonstrations. But unless she understands the movements, she is unlikely to be able to do anything except watch. How do you get her to understand the movements? You give her the right training and opportunities to practice what she's learned.

Realising that we needed to train people was a turning point for me. I was watching people struggling to 'get' the concept of Core Values, often finding myself thinking, 'Yeah, you might know what the values are, but you don't understand them at a deep enough level, or you wouldn't be asking that particular question.'

For instance, we had a value of financial responsibility that didn't mention profit. And yet, people thought, that the point of that particular value was about making profit. It wasn't. It was about being rewarded fairly for what we do, and treating our suppliers fairly. Which in some cases, if we did a bad job, was definitely not about profit, because we shouldn't get paid any profit if we don't do a good job. People were aware of the values, but they didn't understand them.

So, we put together a one-day training course for all the staff. We called it Cracking the Code and used DNA as a metaphor for values. The day had all the usual features you would expect - keynotes, breakout sessions, audio visual presentations. We designed a programme that would keep people interested and engaged while constantly presenting the Core Values to them in different ways to reinforce them and get people to think about them in practical contexts.

The most powerful sessions we did on those days were group discussions where we gave people fictional yet tricky scenarios, to which they needed to apply the Core Values. How do you respond to an anonymous complaint about corruption within a sensitive customer organisation? How do you handle borderline breaches of core values by key managers in high-profile roles? These may sound easy, but we designed the scenarios to be very ambiguous.

Once we presented the scenario, we would ask the group to respond based on their personal views and experience. Without a framework to guide their decisions, people resorted to personal imaginations of what they would or wouldn't do in each scenario. It got pretty heated, with diametrically opposed views on a decision from different individuals, all passionately advocating that they were justified in their answer.

Then we gave them the Core Values and asked them to use these as a framework for making decisions. Right away, we got coherence. We watched as people effortlessly were able to tell us, 'Alright, in this case we would do this, because in our Core Values it says that we should…' They used the actual words in the Core Values statements to interpret what the action in each scenario should be. These group sessions were particularly effective. By making people talk about the values, it forced them to actually think about them. Doing this improved their understanding.

STEP 3: BELIEF

The next stage of getting buy-in is to make people believe, and by implication, trust in, the Values. This is the tricky but crucial stage.

It's all very well doing some booklets, getting some signatures and running a training course. But once people know and then understand the values, how do you get them to actually believe that the values are true for the company?

For most of us to believe something, we want proof. We want proof these values are actually being used: that the CEO believes in and applies them, that the senior executive teams use them, that the operations manager is genuinely bought into the values. People want proof; they want evidence. And the biggest proof that you can give them is to show that your actions are consistent with your words. And both your words and your actions are consistent with your values. This stage of getting buy-in is about authenticity.

This happens most powerfully when people notice you doing things differently because of the values.

Turning down the opportunity to bid for contracts because they did not fit with our values, was a great way of demonstrating our commitment – providing we told our staff about the decision and why we had made it.

Because we included the concept of respect in our core values, we simply couldn't tolerate any form of bullying or harassment.

Because we focused on safety, we could not accept any form of corner-cutting around safety.

Because we had an integrity core value, we had to take action on any concerns around honesty or openness.

Let me give you an example. One of my biggest and most important clients, Shell, asked us to do some consultancy work in the delta area in Nigeria. Shell was a hugely important client, and this was a potentially valuable contract. But after assessing the situation, we realised we couldn't be confident that we could do the contract in line with our safety core value. The kidnapping risk for the area was very high at the time, and we couldn't guarantee that we could satisfy the spirit of our health and safety values. We turned down the opportunity to consult. The client was shocked. 'Your competitors are all willing to do it.'

'Well, I guess that's their choice. But we choose to operate by our Core Values. Sorry.'

It did not damage our relationship with Shell who accepted our position. I suspect it may have even improved it.

We knew that if we weren't consistent, then the game was lost anyway. People will notice if, and when, you apply or fail to apply the values. And this will affect their own personal buy-in more than anything else. You can't switch values off and on, for different days of the week or different clients.

In addition to publicly demonstrating the leadership's application of the values, you need to gather and share proof from other areas of the organisation. Finding proofs and then sharing and repeating them is the only way you're going to get people to believe. And the more proofs you have, the better. This is a long process. It took me two years at least before I got people to actually believe it. Up until that point they were jaded because they'd seen this kind of management 'stuff' before, and it had always fizzled out when a newer initiative was launched.

And so, the only way to ensure that people saw we were serious, was to constantly demonstrate our actions in line with the values and then to tell people about it. And make no mistake, this isn't about all happy-go-lucky and lovey-dovey stuff. Disciplining, or even firing people for breaching the values, is never an easy task.

STEP 4: LIVING THE VALUES

So, once you've got to the point where the Core Values are being applied and communicated consistently throughout the organisation, to the point where people are believing and trusting in them, how do you influence the culture of an organisation so that individuals start to buy-in and live the values themselves?

It will take time. One of the best analogies I've heard of this is from one of my managers in the USA. He was running a marathon for the first time, the Houston Marathon. And he realised that by the time he got to the starting line, there were already people at the first water stop, probably two or three miles down the road, just from the sheer numbers. 'That's like the journey on values,' he said. Don't expect everybody to get to the same point together, don't expect everybody to do it at the same speed. Even two years after starting the journey there are people who haven't even crossed the start line yet; it's a long game. You'll have different people coming through the learning curve at different speeds and at different times, and having that understanding makes all the difference.

You know there's an old cliché that says that culture is the way we do things around here. To change a culture, you need to understand what influences how individuals behave in an organisation. Some of these are:

1. Their own values
2. What they believe the organisation expects and accepts
3. Behaviours, particularly of their colleagues
4. Messages and actions of managers and leaders

5. How their immediate supervisor acts
6. Policies and procedures/rules
7. Reward and pay mechanisms
8. What the culture was yesterday

You cannot really change the first item on the list and you certainly cannot change the last one.

But you can make sure that your organisation's key policies and processes reflect or incorporate your core values. This will include the requirement for people to adhere to, or even promote or champion the core values, and it will be part of your hiring and onboarding processes.

You can also ensure that reward mechanisms align with the values.

That only leaves us with items 2 through 5 – we need to shape the behaviours of leaders, supervisors and colleagues if we expect people to modify their own behaviours, and we need to replace any unhelpful stories or myths about what the organisation used to accept, with a constant stream of new true stories that show exactly what the organisation accepts and expects today. The harvesting, crafting and sharing of these stories is a key role for leaders who want their core values to be real.

As the Leader, you have additional responsibilities:

You are always on show so need to role model the agreed behaviours, demand them of others and openly acknowledge when you slip. People will be watching what you do, the decisions you make, how you talk about things, how you present yourself and how well you listen. You can have a hugely positive impact on making your Core Values work, or you can send out mixed messages that confuse people and erode their trust in you. If you are not optimistic about the future – then who will be? If you don't talk about values and culture all the time, how will people know that you really care about them?

When I talk with company leaders who are frustrated that their teams are not 'getting' the Core Values, invariably the problem lies closer to home. For organisations to truly embrace the power of Core Values they need to use the strength of their team – their whole team. That means embracing diversity of culture, of thought and of gender. Kay Allen will take this further in the next chapter.

And my old boss, Alistair the OIM, never did contact me to tell me if I had made it off his list of people that he felt were poor performers. Presumably there is a faded list somewhere, still stuck under a fridge magnet with my name waiting to be scored off.

ABOUT THE AUTHOR

Bob is passionate about leadership, culture, values and communication and believes that these areas – the 'soft skills' - are really the 'hard' ones that make the difference. His background is in engineering, so he wants to know why things work and how they operate. He is an experienced Chair and CEO of multiple organisations, and has won several awards for entrepreneurship and business leadership.

Bob was responsible for the creation of PSN Ltd (Production Services Network) by manufacturing a $280 million management buyout from Halliburton in 2006, and in April 2011, completed the $1 billion sale of PSN to Wood Group.

He spends four days each week, unpaid, helping organisations in the private, public and third sectors. He likes to remain diversified in his work, assisting large ambitious companies, medium-sized companies that want to grow, and a raft of earlier stage and start-up businesses. He also enjoys his work with several charities, social enterprises and public sector organisations.

He has delivered countless pitches, presentations and talks; winning contracts and raising venture capital for business funding. He claims to have made nearly every mistake possible but is still adding to that list, and often shares his learning in this area with aspiring business leaders. He has developed a unique approach to business storytelling that he is regularly asked to share. Take a look at his TEDx Talk 'Doing Core Values' on YouTube; spot his storyboards and timer on the floor to make sure he finished within 5 seconds of the target time.

A quick snapshot at global gender balance progress shows the gap between men and women, measured in terms of political influence, economic gain and health and education, has narrowed over the last year, but will take another century to disappear, according to the World Economic Forum (WEF).

17

KAY ALLEN

REFRAMING THE GENDER CHALLENGE

I have had the privilege of collaborating with outstanding Chief Executives and C-Suite senior leaders, purposeful people in charge of complex global businesses; leaders with strong values and a desire to leave a legacy for outstanding business performance, within a context of being responsible and ethical.

Successful leaders know that having an authentic, compelling purpose creates a true north for their business direction. Colleagues that are bound together by values enable leaders to deliver on the economics of mutuality[1], building reputational capital based on trust and credibility.

I doubt any CEO would intentionally set a goal of failing, deliberately choosing to ignore personal values, and create a strategy that embeds irresponsible business behaviour into the heart of their company's mission.

When leaders give their teams a greater sense of purpose and a feeling of true inclusion, then employee engagement, loyalty, happiness, and better performance all naturally follow. The challenge for many leaders is that there is often a real gap between their values, a desired ambition, and the reality of present actions.

As a consultant acting as a strategic advisor to senior leaders, my role is to understand why the gap between a desired purpose and what is really happening exists, and then to present solutions to close the gap. I often find myself in the unenviable position of answering the difficult questions and presenting an uncomfortable truth. The answers to the difficult questions often challenge the leader's personal values and undermine their desired purpose.

The awkward admission of low gender balance in senior teams is one of these uncomfortable topics, where even the most purposeful leader appears challenged by the accusation of slow progress.

When a leader asks the question if progress on gender balance can be accelerated, a tentative justification is often presented in ways that try to lay blame on decades of underserved girls not wanting to enter careers that society has conditioned as the domain of men. Plausible explanations can include lack of female desire, lack of skills and lack of applications from women.

A quick snapshot at global gender balance progress shows the gap between men and women, measured in terms of political influence, economic gain and health and education, has narrowed over the last year, but will take another century to disappear, according to the World Economic Forum (WEF).

The WEF[2] predicted it would take 99.5 years for women to be on an equal footing with men, despite women taking high-profile leadership roles at the European Central Bank, the World Bank, and at the head of several countries, including Finland, Germany and New Zealand.

The companies that I have worked with have made great progress in achieving gender balance in feeding the talent pipeline, from early years education to graduate intakes. Progress, however, is still painfully slow at the senior leader and C-Suite level.

In 2019, the proportion of women in senior management roles globally grew to twenty-nine percent. Although, eighty-seven percent of global mid-market companies have just one woman in a senior management role in 2020. Not a great claim to fame, and a lonely place for those successful few.

There has been a great deal of research on why this so called 'gender glass ceiling' exists; an unseen force that secretly prevents women from accelerating their careers to director level.

And yet, all the leaders I have worked with, argue with great passion that they want the best talent and difference of thought in their senior teams, making the connection between diversity of colleagues and customer centricity. Leaders I have spoken to, really understand the power of gender diversity, and many organisations have gender strategies, as well as a range of initiatives designed to nudge the gender percentage dial.

The power gender balance brings is well documented. Research by

McKinsey[3] found those organisations with diverse teams, on average, have 12 percent higher employee productivity; 19 percent higher retention; 57 percent higher team collaboration and 42 percent higher team commitment.

Faced with compelling evidence on the positive impact gender balance brings, and with a public commitment to equality, why does the gender gap persist in the senior echelons of leadership?

To find the true answer, I wanted to work with a leader who was determined to make change faster; a leader that understood real change comes from connecting values and purpose to the power of performance in their organisation.

Sandeep Dadlani agreed to be that leader. He joined Mars, Incorporated in September 2017 as Chief Digital Officer and in 2019 he was named CIO of the year. He understands the absolute necessity for Mars to get closer to consumers. More importantly, Mars wanted to be a digital-first company and having the best possible talent in his teams would be needed in order to accelerate the company's digital transformation. As of January 1, 2020, Mars Digital Technologies had made good progress in driving greater gender balance in the employee talent pipeline, with 28 percent female representation. However, at senior level that representation dropped to 8 percent. Together with his HR Director, Michele Cefola, they applied an agile methodology to ask better questions as to why representation of women was low at senior level. They wanted to really understand what was happening in Mars Digital Technologies that was preventing faster progress to move that stubborn percentage figure. In fact, Sandeep wanted to go 100 times faster, so he needed different solutions.

Sandeep said, "As we set out to build a better world of tomorrow, a world that is consumer-obsessed and digital-first, our biggest learning in addressing gender diversity in our teams was to listen very, very carefully to the end-users. In this case the cohort of 34 amazing women in our teams made us reflect and realize and reframe the problem completely. We then had to let go of the rhetoric and the cliches in this space and begin solving for these problems through a series of agile sprints. At Mars, the consumer is our boss and if at least 50 percent of our consumers are women, listening carefully to our women leaders, becomes even more important than before. I feel privileged to have worked with Michele in beginning to address this imperative in such an innovative way."

Charlotte Sweeney Associates (CSA) is a global leader in providing inclusive leadership strategic advice. As an associate for CSA, I led on the Mars research, along with Katie Gleghorn. Our approach was simple: Let's ask the experts; the women in the employee talent pipeline who were within touching distance of that elusive Vice President grade. Sandeep and Michele invited a very open, ongoing conversation and unfettered access to 34 women in the senior talent pipeline. They had no influence over the questions we asked and had no input into the report. This was a brave and innovative approach. An approach that Sandeep believed in passionately, asking the right questions to find the right solutions, even if that meant hearing some difficult feedback.

34 senior women all took part in confidential interviews which remained anonymous in the final report. The findings were brutal in their honesty, humbling in their sincerity, and powerful in identifying why gender balance was failing to materialise in senior roles in Mars Digital Technologies.

One quote from a Mars female associate set the tone for the way forward. "If we really get close to the problems women face, we can reframe the gender challenge but only if Mars is truly bold enough to throw out the rule book and let an iterative process begin to find brand new solutions."

This was the key. To find new solutions to an age-old problem. The research sought to understand Mars Digital Technologies women Associates' needs, challenge assumptions, redefine problems and create innovative ideas to take forward as part of a design thinking approach.

The findings of the research demonstrated that women participants had an incredible array of qualifications and experiences and they were all very clear that they wanted to progress. Ambition to succeed literally shone through the interviews. The conclusion: the desire to become a senior leader was definitely not the blocker for this cohort of women.

What the women questioned for themselves was how they should go about realising this ambition? This cohort of women surfaced a challenge for themselves, how to articulate, pursue and realise ambition.

The research found that Mars Digital Technologies had put in place all the actions you would expect to find in a progressive gender action plan. The employee value proposition was strong. Mars Associates referenced superb policies and benefits, great flexible working and a very collaborative culture.

What did emerge were four core gender challenge themes, which revealed what the women believed acted as enablers and barriers for progressing senior careers.

These were:

1. Career Ownership
2. Harnessing Support
3. Inclusive Leadership
4. The Mars Influence

Owning one's career was called out as one of the big enablers and barriers to career progression. This was a multifaceted issue. The complexity of the gender challenges ranged from ambiguity around career pathways, lack of structure for development plans, and a lack of focus on personal development with a big emphasis on softer skill development. This was compounded by the struggle to get noticed and raise one's visibility. And yet, as mentioned above, there was definitely no shortage of ambition and career aspiration within the women interviewed.

The barrier seemed to be more about knowing how to continue to develop personally, frame ambition, showcase passion and have the confidence to pursue a senior career pathway.

Several of the Associates had really grasped this challenge. They knew how to leverage sponsorship, use networks, focus on learning and how to seek out opportunities. The insights from these women could really help design a transparent approach to the employee talent pipeline; to create a leadership development programme, and open up access for more women to push through the barrier of middle management to more senior positions.

Feminine behaviour traits were frequently discussed in the interviews as perceived self-limiting barriers; how women feel about networking, pay negotiation, needing feedback and how they seek recognition. The Mars Associates did have self-belief and confidence. However, how they pushed themselves forward compared to men was an issue that held women back. Several of the Associates talked about past role models, mentors and family members who had raised this issue of taking control and being more intentional about pushing forward. A word used a great deal was 'intentionality' however, there seemed a disconnect between knowing you had to push yourself forward and actually doing it.

How to tell your story, and building on your career to date with a forward aspirational goal, is a skill women don't seem to spend time developing. Sandeep and Michele decided to give their associates the space and freedom to develop this skill.

The cohort shares their insights on what they would do if they could design a talent programme to accelerate progress and deliver better gender balance. The research concluded a 12-point action plan to accelerate change to achieve gender balance at the senior leadership level.

O W N E R S H I P	Be proud of the talent in the pipeline, improve visibility and transparency and communicate what it means to be recognised as talent	Showcase and role model career pathways, have more proactive discussions on career aspirations and how to take career ownership	Design a female leadership programme which enables women to focus on themselves and develop softer skills
H A R N E S S S U P P O R T	Communicate to male colleagues the essential role they play especially in being sponsors and mentors	Enable women to seek a career coach to help define, pursue and realise career ambition. Legitimise space and time for this process	Create a women's network to facilitate networking and personal support, creating a gender expert panel inside Mars

L E A D E R S H I P	Capitalise on the influence of senior leaders to change the behaviour at middle management	Focus on delivering a management training programme that focuses on inclusive leadership and unconscious bias	Look to showcase role models ensuring Mars shines a light on its own role models – Share stories and portray women as leaders
M A R S I N F L U E N C E	Set up a project to capture smart gender data which can be published and analysed – this should include gender pay	Focus on attraction and selection driving female talent into and through the talent pipeline	Look at reframing how Maternity leave is managed – introducing unique self governance for maternity leave cover which supports talent growth

Sandeep took an incredibly bold next step. The research findings were presented to the Mars Digital Technologies senior leadership team in a webinar, with the women participants all taking part in the meeting. The initial reaction was profound. It was profound because the findings challenged the purpose and values of each member of the leadership team. No one enjoyed hearing the uncomfortable truth that they were the current leaders of an organisation where women felt undervalued.

This case study is a powerful example of how leaders who have strong values and clear purpose focused on diversity and inclusion, can create a seismic shift in gender balance at senior leadership. Sandeep Dadlani had the confidence to really get close to the problems women face, enabling him to be bold enough to throw out the rule book and let the women of Mars Digital

Technologies deliver new ways of tackling the gender imbalance. Sandeep of course knows the business and moral case for driving this agenda, but he also has a deep personal value as the father of daughters who are ready to pursue their careers. He wants to ensure they have no barriers in front of them.

Sandeep commented on the webinar, "Every day at dinner, my teenage daughters amaze me with their brilliant insights of happenings during the day. Mars being a family company, we decided to take the same "family" approach to listening very, very carefully to our amazing women leaders. What we found was brilliant, inspiring and surprising! The rhetoric and cliches were gone and we started solving specific problems for our end-users. Not just for our amazing women leaders but for our amazing women consumers as well. This approach has encouraged Michele and I to drive this movement of addressing gender balance with more passion than ever."

There are several key insights from this research that others can apply:

Research the real challenges. This will be different for different types of organisations, sectors and size of business. You already employ the experts; talk to women colleagues, delve into their challenges and really listen to their concerns. This type of honest research can help you identify the things that women have personally experienced that influence career progress to senior levels. There are many complex factors that create the glass ceiling, but we can't deny its existence is real.

Take action from top. I truly believe that only a CEO-led effort to change the organisation to a gender equal one, will be effective. It should be like introducing any transformational management approach, such as TQM or lean manufacturing. A CEO must be fully committed and make parity a priority. Policy changes that facilitate equal opportunities for women leaders are, of course, important, as are enabling strategies, employee groups and affinity networks. However, a change in belief comes from the leader.

Empower women to take ownership of their career. Helping female leaders to embrace the skills and push for these changes at an individual level. Coaching on the power of strategic networking and on the importance of storytelling, or how to communicate and pitch ideas in a compelling way. All of these skills are learnt, enabling women to have the confidence to own their career pathway.

Permission to be visible. Creating the permissive culture to invest in oneself, to take valuable time to create a personal brand narrative, and to pay attention on becoming visible. Visibility of female talent to the senior leadership team is vital. Coaching, mentoring and sponsorship help women to navigate the labyrinth of senior appointments. The tone that the leader sets creates the confidence to be visible.

There was no one specific issue creating the gender imbalance at senior leadership levels that Mars Digital Technologies could easily address. No magic bullet. The conversations felt like a labyrinth of interconnecting cause and effect issues: having space and time to develop a clear understanding of their value set, defining career ambition, articulating a development plan with a mentor, and getting noticed by a sponsor. This maze was compounded by inconsistent leadership development, soft skill development and the idea of self-promotion enabling intentionality around career ownership.

Sandeep and Michele are now empowering a visible talent pipeline, placing a strong focus on self-development and personal career ownership.

In conclusion, this research demonstrates that leaders who take a purposeful perspective of building an inclusive culture, will see innovation thrive. There now needs to be a leader's rebellion against a gender gap that will not close on its own – it needs purposeful leaders to take action now. The evidence is compelling, the solutions available, the benefits waiting to deliver.

ENDNOTES

1   https://www.sbs.ox.ac.uk/sites/default/files/2018-06/MiB-EoM_
Backgrounder_6.6.15.pdf

2   https://www.weforum.org/reports/gender-gap-2020-report-100-
years-pay-equality

3   https://www.mckinsey.com/featured-insights/diversity-and-
inclusion/women-in-the-workplace

ABOUT THE AUTHOR

Kay's passion is to develop responsible business and diversity & inclusion strategies that uncover the truth behind company barriers and enablers, with in-depth meaningful research.

Her purpose is to help others succeed: As a coach, she loves to draw on past experience, helping others to grow and develop by using their unique talents. With 25 years providing advice to business, ensuring integrity, inclusion and sustainability are at the core of business growth plans, Kay supported Prime Minster Cameron and the campaign 'Every Business Commits' looking at how businesses can help local communities, driving greater social responsibility as part of the Big Society.

Kay is a past Fellow of St Georges House Windsor, A Fellow of the Chartered Institute of Personnel and Development and a Fellow of the Royal Society of Arts. She has been listed in Who's Who since 2010.

Kay has worked for B&Q, BSKYB and Royal Mail. She has been a Commissioner on the Disability Rights Commission and the Equality and Human Rights Commission. She also served as a Non-Executive Director on the Department for Work and Pensions PDCS Board.

She was awarded an OBE for services to Equality in 2010.

Currently Kay is a Strategic Advisor to PurpleSpace and works with Charlotte Sweeney Associates. She serves as a panel member on Ofcom's Communications Consumer Panel.

She is a published Author: 'Corporates are from Mars; Charities are from Venus'

Something called 'innovation' is arguably essential to thriving in a low-certainty, high-complexity environment. Let's define innovation for this chapter as bringing 'meaningfully unique' ideas to life; whether these are internal business improvements or new services or products, innovations need to be both 'new & different' and of sufficient value to the organisation and its target market.

PHILIP POZZO DI BORGO-OLIVER

18 PURPOSEFUL INNOVATION:

making the most of people's talent and
diversity, even in difficult times

I'm looking at a black and white photograph of my father. He has one foot perched on a railing while he leans over a sturdy wooden bridge, feeding a pair of swans jostling for position on the sparkling river below.

If you were able to peek over my shoulder, you would notice that this is not a snap from a family outing; he's wearing 'action working dress', South African Navy issue. And I know the photograph is taken by one of his men.

When I was little, Dad would periodically disappear for a few weeks with his unit into the wilderness on survival exercises that he would spring on them; climbing mountains, building rafts, living off the land and generally trying not to kill anyone while teaching them essential team and leadership lessons along the way.

The sea was his great love; first as a Royal Navy diver, then as a torpedo anti-submarine officer. When he arrived in Simonstown during the mid-70's on an expatriate commission with his young family, this African navy offered lots of opportunities for a dynamic leader with a passion for trying new things.

As a strict commanding officer, he didn't suffer fools, but at home I knew the Commander as a man with a wicked sense of humour and a creative mind.

He never laughed away my childhood projects. When I salvaged an old kitchen cupboard, up-ended it to make a vertical shelf unit, packed it with my own story books and encyclopaedias and rented them out at five cents per week to my mates, Dad just winked and nodded his encouragement. It wasn't a great success, but it was fun, and I learned a few early lessons about business.

He actively encouraged me to give things a go. My father made it safe for me to try, and safe to fail. His strong sense of occasion meant that I could always look forward to several thoughtful paragraphs in a letter or card to congratulate me on my achievements.

These days, I work with leaders and entrepreneurs who need to create the same kind of enabling culture in their organisations. They want to know how best to think up new product and service concepts, and how to make those concepts come alive. They know they need to create some kind of 'innovation culture', but they're not sure what that really looks like or what their role should be in making it happen.

We face a world in change and crisis like never before.

On the one hand, we are mesmerized by the extraordinary technologies unfolding before us: artificial intelligence, blockchain, cyber currencies, and all the advances in alternative energy production and storage. By contrast, a global pandemic has upturned lives and business models in equal measure, as if the climate change crisis wasn't a big enough challenge already.

In a business context, a crisis is often an opportunity to be capitalised on. Put differently, organisations capable of reinventing themselves are likely to be resilient in the face of economic downturns. Independent research conducted by the Innovation Engineering Institute on behalf of the US Department of Commerce[1] illustrates this fact in stark terms: between 2008 and 2011, organisations with an established innovation system were shown to outperform their peers during the last financial crisis by an average of 80 percentage points in sales growth, and eighty-three percentage points in increased profitability.

The business community instinctively knows the importance of being able to bring new ideas to market quickly and efficiently. A Price Waterhouse Coopers' annual study[2] lists the 'innovation skill gap' as the number one concern of global CEOs. This same priority is also reflected in the World Economic Forum 'Future of Jobs' report on the most important skills for 2025[3]: of those ranked in the top ten, each skill can be mapped back to the kinds of creative, communication, and commercialisation capabilities that have been shown to drive effective innovation.

INNOVATION IS KEY

So, something called 'innovation' is arguably essential to thriving in a low-certainty, high-complexity environment. Let's define innovation for this chapter as bringing 'meaningfully unique' ideas[4] to life; whether these are internal business improvements or new services or products, innovations need to be both 'new & different' and of sufficient value to the organisation and its target market.

But delivering innovations consistently and repeatedly well takes more than luck and a few clever folk working in a dark room somewhere in the organisation.

The arc of my professional career has taken me from engineering-based problem solving to business improvement, via team and leadership coaching. In my last corporate role in a major energy services company, I was innovation manager for their asset solutions division. I've lived through the pain and challenges of trying to drive innovation in the absence of a proven method for innovating, and within an industry culture that is often resistant to fresh thinking.

Nowadays, with the benefit of hindsight, advanced innovation studies, and as a practitioner of a proven system for high-impact innovation, I'm better able to appreciate this experience and understand how we might have done it rather differently. In fact, leaders (organisations) don't really know *how* to innovate consistently: a McKinsey Quarterly study[5] reveals that almost two thirds of leaders lack confidence in their organisation's ability to be innovative - despite what they tell the world to the contrary on their websites!

KEEPING INNOVATION GOING IS HARD WITHOUT THE CULTURE TO SUPPORT IT

But there's another challenge on the horizon. As organisations become less like regimented barracks of same-thinking people looking for tenure, relying on time-served 'experts' to hold things together will become less feasible. Organisations will no longer be able to lean on individual know-how to keep the show running.

This means that getting organisational culture 'right' is going to be even more important. In fact, building an innovative culture is among the top three most pressing internal concerns of global CEOs surveyed by The Conference Board[6]. This is especially vital in the remote-working world that we have all been tipped into during 2020. Forbes magazine put this warning starkly[7]: 'If there's an organisational culture lesson that's coming out of this pandemic, it's that what was bad in a culture before is most likely doubly bad when remote.'

As management theorist and systems thinker W. Edwards Deming explained, when he was helping Japan to revolutionise its post-WWII car production: 94% of problems in an enterprise are attributable to the system itself, and only 6% to the individuals working within it. The urgent implication of Deming's observation is that we must design and redesign our organisational cultures carefully and intentionally. A recent example of building a 'culture-first' organisation is the French health insurance industry disruptor, *Alan.com*[8], created by Jean-Charles Samuelian-Werve and his co-founders. Their entire business is designed around the work culture and values[9] they believe their employees and customers are looking for: high-trust, easy to do business with, simple to understand.

So, if innovation is so important, and building a culture of innovation is essential to innovate sustainably, *how* should we do it, and what is the role of *leadership* in all this?

THERE IS HOPE FOR PURPOSEFUL INNOVATION

Is there a magic formula or secret recipe to leading and nurturing 'purposeful' innovation? Is there a way of doing innovation that is intentional, by design, something around which an organisation can be rallied - something that isn't hit or miss, doesn't rely on a guru or a few hard-working folk, but actually can be learned, practised and embedded into the DNA of an organisation?

It turns out there is. My partners and I have built our Eureka!Europe innovation coaching and training consultancy around this. We see, close-up, the measurable benefits of using a proven, evidence-based approach to purposeful innovation that elegantly answers these questions.

Serial inventor Doug Hall spent two years working with teams to identify what actually drives the generation of 'meaningfully unique' ideas in the real world[10]. He figured out that three key factors make this possible:
1. stimulus for ideas (to feed your brain)
2. diversity of thinking
3. minimising fear

Doug realised that effective innovation takes place in an environment – a culture – where all three principles are respected and managed. He developed the equation in **Fig. 1** to explain how these factors drive and sustain innovation.

$$\text{Effective Innovation} = \frac{\text{idea STIMULUS} \times \text{DIVERSITY of thinking}}{\text{driving out FEAR}}$$

Figure 1: The ingredients for purposeful, effective innovation

So what does this diagram tell us? In simple terms, we can say that effective innovation (or purposeful innovation, in the way I described it earlier) is directly proportional to the amount of idea stimulus provided, boosted exponentially by the diversity of thinking applied, and diminished by the degree to which fear is present.

LET'S UNPACK EACH FACTOR A LITTLE FURTHER:

- **Stimulus** is about introducing 'trigger' ideas. These ideas may be related to your potential market, competitors, emerging technology, or patents, but might equally be concepts or trends completely unrelated to the innovation focus. It's about learning. This is 'open innovation' territory; a technique made famous by Henry Chesbrough[11] to leverage solutions and concepts from other industries and sources. Actively seeking out stimulus promotes a healthy culture of learning[12].
- If stimulus is the spark and flame, **diversity** is the fuel to stoke the creative engine. When you bring in different perspectives, experiences and ways of thinking, the ideas generated become more interesting, more unusual, less predictable - 'bigger and bolder'. Effective innovation demands a blend of genders[13], cultures, hierarchies, education, and thinking styles - it's about collaboration[14] in the widest sense of the word.
- A little creative tension is a good thing, but the kind of **fear** that discourages people[15] from trying anything new or different is not helpful, and it poisons the pioneer spirit. If an organisation doesn't value structured experimentation as a means of learning (and thereby improving), then it's extremely hard to encourage innovation. In that kind of culture, only 'safe bets' or copycat ideas can make it through the system.

LEADERSHIP MAKES ALL THE DIFFERENCE

There is more to the model in **Fig. 1** than might be apparent at first glance.

By slightly elaborating the diagram, see **Fig. 2**, the same model also elegantly explains how organisational learning, collaboration and experimentation drive innovation, and the vital role of leadership in establishing and nurturing a culture of innovation.

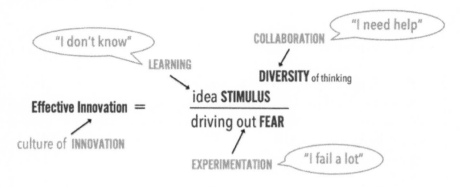

Figure 2: Innovation from a culture and leadership perspective.

Importantly, the callout bubbles in this diagram echo the kinds of things you might have heard some leaders say before: 'I don't have all the answers…'; 'I don't always get it right…'; 'I need your help to make this happen.'

These words are not incidental. They are in the fabric of leadership[16], in the deep tissue of leading: it is the language of humility, wisdom, and trust. The leader who can say these things honestly will gain the respect of her people and sow the seeds of a culture of learning, collaboration and experimentation, the essential ingredients for effective innovation that Doug Hall uncovered in his research.

SOME THINGS I'VE LEARNED ABOUT PURPOSEFUL INNOVATION

In the absence of a system for innovating, organisational innovation is serendipitous or accidental. Or it relies on the hard work of a 'gifted few' to keep it going (and what happens once they move on?). I don't think that's much of a business strategy, and I would argue that it's disrespectful of the organisation's talent.

I wish I'd known when I was a corporate innovation manager some years ago, what I know now; I would have been able to drive much more powerful innovation, at pace. And it could have been sustainable.

Hindsight is a wonderful thing, but perhaps I can share a few things I've learned along the way, which I hope this chapter has begun to clarify for you:

- Innovation is a skill and capability that is much needed and much talked about. Organisations that are proactive, systematic innovators are better off, especially during tough times.
- Whilst there are few proven approaches to innovating consistently, and much innovation is confused with high technology or digitalisation, the approach to innovation I've been talking about is purposeful, systemic, and systematic.
- More importantly, the innovation model we've touched on provides practical guidance to leaders who really want to make the most of the diverse talent and experience in their organisations.
- Anyone can learn to innovate, and the right innovation approach can leverage diversity of thinking, reduce fear of experimenting, and push the creative edge of the concepts generated.
- Your leadership plays a vital role in enabling innovation and designing the future that your organisation needs.

REFLECTION

That photograph of my father reminds me where my sense of curiosity comes from. Dad didn't make me an inventor and I am only in the foothills of my own journey into the land of innovation, but his encouragement and respect for my ideas, meant that I grew up believing in the value of trying new things; he created a safe space that supported 'innovation', even though he may not have realised it at the time.

What does a culture of supportive experimentation do for an organisation? It motivates people to try. It makes you resilient: you can pick yourself up, dust yourself off, pause to consider what you've learned and what you'll do differently, and after a deep breath you take another step forward with a spirit of productive curiosity.

My own experiences of working with leaders and teams, in organisations both big and small, tell me that we can make much more of the talent and diversity that comes to work everyday. People *want* to make meaningful contributions and share what they know to build a better product, or create valuable new things. People want to be purposeful. They just need to know how, and have a safe space to try. They need a culture of innovation.

Pioneers like Doug Hall have shown what it takes to build and sustain a system-wide culture for effective innovation[17]. It isn't rocket science, but it *is* scientific.

The challenges we face today - climactic, political, technological, cultural, and medical - need fresh thinking and new perspectives. Finding intelligent and sustainable solutions need not be left to chance. If ever there was a right time for businesses and institutions to be purposeful about innovating, surely it is now.

Ultimately, leadership is the all-enabling force that will shape your workplace culture into something generative, positive and productive. Or not. The good news is that your culture of innovation, whatever it looks like now, can be changed, and the levers of that change are known and within reach.

ACKNOWLEDGEMENTS

I would like to acknowledge and thank:
- Doug Hall and the Innovation Engineering Institute for allowing the use of original research and proprietary models throughout this chapter, in particular the 'effective innovation' equation referenced in Figures 1 and 2.
- Helen Potter and Dougie Potter for their friendship, support and steadfast partnership as co-founders with me of Eureka!Europe LLP.
- My wife, Julia Ann Krone for her proofreading and helpful encouragement.
- Chris Paton and all my collaborators on this amazing project - thank you for your inspiring stories and vision.

ENDNOTES

1   Further information on this report for the US Dept. of Commerce is available upon request from Eureka!Europe LLP (email: connect@eureka1europe.com)

2   Price Waterhouse Coopers (2019). 22nd Annual Global CEO Survey: 'What do CEOs know about the future?' Online report. Available at: https://www.pwc.com/gx/en/ceo-survey/2019/report/pwc-22nd-annual-global-ceo-survey.pdf (accessed: March 2020)

3   World Economic Forum. 'Future of Jobs Report'. Online Report. Available at: https://www.weforum.org/reports/the-future-of-jobs-report-2020 (accessed: October 2020)

4   I am referring here to Innovation Engineering®, a practical approach to innovation developed by Doug Hall over more than 35 years and used by organisations across the world. My business partners and I at Eureka!Europe LLP (www.eureka1europe.com) are licensees of the Innovation Engineering Institute. We train, coach and consult using Doug's methods.

5   The McKinsey Quarterly: Barsh, J., Capozzi, M., and Davidson, J. (2008). Leadership and Innovation. Online report. Available at: https://www.mckinsey.com/business-functions/strategy-and-corporate-finance/our-insights/leadership-and-innovation (accessed: March 2020)

6   The Conference Board (2020). C-Suite Challenge 2020: Collaborating to Compete. Online report available at: https://www.conference-board.org/topics/c-suite-challenge (accessed: March 2020).

7   Forbes (2020): Gostick, A. '5 Ways To Build Better Remote Work Cultures' Online article. Available at: https://www.forbes.com/sites/adriangostick/2020/10/06/5-ways-to-build-better-remote-work-cultures/?utm_=newsletter&utmemail&utm_=thememo&cdlcid=5e1e1a19a806e27817edf98b#3ebbc10b57ef (accessed: October 2020)

8   For a fascinating look under the bonnet of Alan, I'd urge you to read 'Healthy Business' by Samuelian-Werve. Available at: https://alan.com/livre-healthy-business.

9   Elsewhere in this book, Bob Keiller takes a personal look at the role of values in shaping and leading organisations.

10   Doug and his lead researcher, Dr. Chris Stormann, modelled this experimental data with high statistical confidence; the fascinating results can be read in 'Jump Start Your Business Brain' (Brain Brew Books, 2001).

11   See Henry Chesbrough's 'Open Innovation' (Harvard Business

School Press, 2006)

12   Elsewhere in this book, Chris McKibbin explores how you can access expert knowledge by building networks of networks.

13   Elsewhere in this book, read Kay Allen's thoughts on balancing thinking and perspectives with gender diversity.

14   Elsewhere in this book, Kanishka Misal explores collaboration and partnerships - the power of working as an ecosystem.

15   Elsewhere in this book, read about Dom Hawes' notion of 'makers and takers - how to encourage experimentation when the culture doesn't easily support it. See also Chris Paton's chapter on leveraging diversity of thinking by creating safe spaces for 'helpful disagreement'.

16   I really like the Future-Engage-Deliver or FED model articulated brilliantly by its originator, Steve Radcliffe, in his book 'Leadership Plain and Simple' (FT Publishing, 2012). His uncomplicated but powerful approach invites us to describe the future, engage people in it, and then relentlessly support them to deliver. It focuses not only on the destination but also the journey. Elsewhere in this book, Keith Holdt offers another perspective on leadership with the 'Captain's Voyage' framework.

17   You can discover for yourself the backstory, theory and practice of Doug Hall's Innovation Engineering® approach in his latest book, 'Driving Eureka!' (Cleristy Press, 2018)

ABOUT THE AUTHOR

Born into an English-French family, Philip grew up on three continents, leaving him with a keen sense of curiosity about culture and a desire to explore 'what's over the hill.' From Singapore to Cape Town and a dozen cities in between, he describes his working life as mix of technical and creative roles, with a constant theme of wanting to change and improve things, woven through it all.

He believes that's what attracts him to these lines from TS Elliot: 'We shall not cease from exploration, and the end of all our exploring will be to arrive where we started and know the place for the first time.'

Philip has been mildly obsessed with helping operational teams work smarter since he was a young team leader helping pioneer the mining of diamonds, with De Beers off the coast of Southern Africa. A university educated engineer and systems practitioner, Philip has had several corporate roles in transformational change, leadership development and innovation. Clients and colleagues have described him as pioneering, spirited, and a gifted out-of-the-box thinker with professional integrity.

As a founding partner or Eureka! Europe LLP (www.eureka1europe.com) and a black belt Innovation Engineer-in-training, Philip continues his creative journey with business partners Helen Potter and Dougie Potter. Together, they teach and coach a proven innovation method that enables leaders to develop their teams to become smarter innovators, build innovation muscle, and grow their businesses.

Nothing energises Philip more than seeing people light up with fresh insights: 'I believe leaders have a duty to make the most of their team's energy and creativity. My job, is to help organisations learn smarter with more innovative ways of thinking, communicating and working.'

Philip enjoys writing poetry, plays golf moderately badly, and recovers by practicing yoga. He lives in Edinburgh, and is married to the inspiring and talented artist, Julia Krone, who shares a passion for swimming and travel. Philip is also proud father to Haydn, who, like so many, is currently making sense of being a university student in a topsy-turvy Covid-19 world.

Having lost an uncle and brother to cancer, Philip is delighted that 'Purposeful People' will be helping to raise funds for Cancer Fund for

Children (https://cancerfundforchildren.com/), along with three other very worthy charities.

Contact Phil if you'd like to talk innovation, organisational culture change, poetry, or anything else you think you might have a great conversation about!

- Email philip.oliver@eureka1europe.com
- LinkedIn www.linkedin.com/in/philipoliver

Being clear about the destination, whether it's how much you want the business to be worth or what you want your sales to be, is the starting point for building a plan to get there. It's equally as important that every member of the senior leadership team has a clear understanding of the goal and believes that the destination is achievable.

19

KEITH HOLDT

YOU ARE THE CAPTAIN OF YOUR SHIP

Gerry was the CEO of a software business where we'd just invested £50m; a sizeable investment for the mid-market private equity firm I was working with. A sales-focused CEO, he'd built the business over a 5-year period, leading with energy, enthusiasm and charisma. Recently he had taken the previously listed business private and had led the acquisition of a business in Australia, expanding their business empire. I was sitting opposite him now. He looked at me through black-rimmed spectacles as he leaned back in a leather chair, arms folded, almost challenging me to see how much I knew.

"Tell me what you do," I asked.

An hour later, he was still talking, and I was getting increasingly worried. Nothing he had said was clear, or simple. The more he talked, the more complexity he introduced. My concerns were growing by the minute.

My role in the private equity firm was to work with investee businesses to build and implement plans that would ensure that the expected returns were delivered. Over years of working as an engineer, management consultant and in corporate roles around the world, I have found that asking the simple question, "Tell me what you do?" can be one of the quickest ways to understand whether a CEO is on top of their game...or not. If the answer is unclear and long-winded, more often than not, the business will have challenges.

I left the meeting and told the investment director that I thought the business was going to have real problems. There was some incredulity, after all, hadn't we just completed very detailed due diligence? Within 6 months, the business was weeks away from running out of cash and in turnaround. Four years, a lot of hard work and a new executive team later, we barely made our money back.

Private Equity investors don't want to wait forever for their returns, and the mantra for investing is 'Buy Low, Good Management Team, Sell High'. This is a world where the rubber hits the road. Management teams need to deliver or often find themselves looking for new pastures. In particular, the CEOs of these businesses often find themselves under significant pressure, having to deliver against plans month after month to meet expectations. Out of every 10 investments, 2-3 typically perform poorly, 4-5 will make plan, and only 2-3 will achieve exceptional results.

As I've come to learn over my thirty-year career, great businesses have one key thing in common; they are led by exceptional CEOs. CEOs with total FOCUS on the results they need to achieve and the people involved, to build a great business. CEOs with PACE, always moving forward, whether fast or slow, and doing something to add value to the business. CEOs with the DISCIPLINE to keep going through the ups and the downs.

Ben, CEO of a provider of luxury log cabin holidays, another recent private equity investment, was one such exceptional CEO. The business' head office was located in a tiny English village, and, as I walked through the door on my first visit, I was met by Ben who ushered me into the board room. As usual I asked the question, "Tell me what you do?" Within 5 minutes Ben clearly explained their proposition. I had no doubts as to why they had been successful. Straight away his focus moved to the plan and what needed to be done.

Working with other businesses, I quickly realised that not all CEOs and management teams were this focused. Many struggled to get going, others felt the pressure to deliver results. My big question – was there a way to get teams focused, disciplined and moving, and to do this repeatedly and consistently across many different businesses?

This was brought to a head one day when working with a different management team. The chairman, getting frustrated at the lack of focus, turned to them and said, "Take careful note, this is the difference between a second house in Wales and a yacht on the Caribbean". The idea of a yacht on the Caribbean took hold, and I said to the team, "Actually, running your business is much like a captain sailing his ship." The metaphor became the basis for the answer to my big question. It shaped a simple framework for building a focused strategy that delivers results. I call it "The Captain's Voyage".

SO, WHAT DOES A CAPTAIN NEED TO HAVE A SUCCESSFUL VOYAGE?

1. THE RIGHT CARGO:

In a business this is what you have to sell. It's this simple - is what you have to sell easy for your sellers to sell and for your customers to buy? It is why the question "Tell me what you do?" is so important, and why the answer means everything.

I am always amazed by how often I don't get a clear answer when I ask CEOs this question. I put myself in the position of a customer and ask myself "Is it making sense? Is there a clear reason why I would pay for this?" It is often the place my work with a business begins. I ask the CEO to explain the business to me as if I were a 10-year-old, and I ask myself whether the 10-year-old in me would get it.

Ben's answer was clear and simple. "We sell luxury holiday experiences in log cabins with hot tubs set in beautiful forests." It didn't even take 5 minutes for me to know I wanted to experience one of these holidays.

As I got to know his business more, it was clear that this clarity was pervasive and consistent throughout the business. On the website, in their brochures, through all the sales channels, through to every staff member. And when I spoke to customers, they got it too and quickly became raving evangelists, the ultimate tick in the box!

The simpler the message is, the easier it is to get the business aligned behind it, for sales people to sell the product, and for customers to buy it.

Successful, purpose-driven business leaders need to work on their product and their offer until the value it brings is clear and simple to all.

2. THE CO-ORDINATES OF HIS DESTINATION:

In private equity backed businesses, a target valuation and time are a clear destination, but they are no less important for every business, whether private equity backed or not. A focused business leader will be clear about their destination, their targets and what they are looking to achieve.

When I began working with Ben, we'd just invested at a valuation of a little over £10m. We were looking to achieve a valuation of over £90m within 4 years; a big increase from the onset.

Being clear about the destination, whether it's how much you want the business to be worth or what you want your sales to be, is the starting point for building a plan to get there. It's equally as important that every member of the senior leadership team has a clear understanding of the goal and believes that the destination is achievable.

As Ben and I discussed his targets, we chatted about how using the value of 1% of the business value to track the journey simply was an easy way to show each member of the leadership team what their efforts would be worth.

Ben immediately decided to take his team away for a weekend to plan their journey. He asked them if they'd be happy with what their stake would be worth at the end of 4 years should they achieve the plan they'd signed up to with the private equity investors. They all agreed that they'd prefer to hit a higher target, even though the targets were already challenging. This focused their minds and ensured they were all aligned as they began to update their plan to achieve greater goals.

Once the destination is clear, it becomes easier to determine whether you have a product or service that is viable and what steps are necessary to reach one's intended destination.

Successful, purpose driven business leaders have a clear destination in mind. They are supported by team members who are determined to reach the chosen destination.

3. A CLEAR ROUTE:

There is never only one way to reach a destination, but it is important to choose a route and get sailing.

Different routes have different risks and opportunities, which all need to be considered. After such consideration, the chosen route should give you the best chance of arriving at your destination.

This means asking questions like:

Which customers are most likely to buy, and where are they?

Which sales channels are they most likely to use to buy?

Is there an untapped market, and is this an opportunity or a diversion?

Are there any risks, such as political risk and uncertainty, that could affect us?

Are you going for speed, or ease?

Who are the competition, and do they pose a threat?

When we invested in Ben's company the business already had a number of sites spread out in forests across the United Kingdom. It was identified early on that a key driver for building the value of the business would be the development of new sites and increasing the capacity of existing sites. Much thought went into planning the locations of these sites, ensuring that each would be able to tap into their target market. One key risk identified was getting planning permission for each of the sites early on, so plans were put in place to manage this closely. Another risk was ensuring that sufficient funding was available to do the site development, which was put in place up front.

Careful planning of the route to your destination can be the difference between success and failure, and successful business leaders are only too aware of this. Of course, this doesn't mean that the route can't be changed along the way should unforeseen opportunities or risks arise. However, setting sail without a clear plan of how to reach the desired destination can lead to disaster.

Successful, purpose-driven business leaders know the route they plan to take, and are focused on sailing it, making the most of opportunities that come their way, and taking steps to avoid any risks.

4. A SHIP THAT IS CAPABLE OF THE JOURNEY:

Your current business is the ship that got you to where you are today, but this doesn't mean it's ready for the voyage ahead.

Can it get there fast enough?

Where can it be streamlined?

Does it need new capabilities, systems or processes?

Ben focused on a number of important areas in the holiday business. He knew he needed to work on pricing, and to focus on getting better margins, which meant going through every aspect of the business to streamline costs.

He set targets for increasing the spend per head per booked night and looked to double this from £16 per head to £30. He put plans in place to improve returns on online investment; expanding their audience and building a loyal customer base. He left nothing to chance. He had his key numbers at his fingertips, such as the current occupancy levels and spend per night, and he was constantly looking for ways to improve them.

Building a business can be hard but it doesn't need to be complicated. The simpler the business, the easier it is to build and grow, and the easier it becomes to navigate the journey.

To make solid progress, you may need to change your processes. You may need to change your structure. You may even need to buy other businesses. Sometimes you may even need to start again.

Successful, purpose-driven CEOs constantly monitor and fine-tune their ship, whilst keeping track of key performance metrics.

5. THE RIGHT CREW:

It's no good setting sail in a cruise liner when the crew you have on board have only ever sailed a row boat. No matter how prepared you may be, every ship will flounder if it has the wrong crew in the wrong place.

This can be difficult to achieve, but it is the single most important thing in a business and can mean the difference between success and failure. Every successful CEO I have worked with prioritises this point and selects team members who possess the right skills and attitude. You may need to hire new people to fill gaps you didn't know you had or move existing people into different roles that better suit their skills. You may even need to get rid of a few. The best business leaders will be single-minded about finding the right people to fill the right positions to ensure smooth sailing.

Ben surrounded himself with a great team. He had a strong Finance Director, who he could trust with taking care of the numbers, and a strong Marketing Director who single-mindedly focused on expanding their market penetration. Furthermore, he brought on an ex-military man to oversee the site expansion.

I have found that often the best place to start is to draw an organisation chart, with no names, that represents your ideal business structure. Next, start filling in the blanks with the names of your current team, before finally working out a plan to fill in the gaps.

Also important is to identify the dependencies, starting with yourself. Ask the questions, "Could the ship keep sailing without me?" and "If anything happened to any of my team, what are the implications?" We all like to feel indispensable, but a ship that depends on one person is in dangerous waters.

Ben was a great CEO, and surrounded himself with a good team, but he took care to put structures in place to ensure that the business wouldn't fail by being too dependent on one person; himself included.

Successful, purpose driven business leaders surround themselves with the right crew and ensure they are in the right place at the right time. A great crew on a poor ship still gives you every chance of success, but a poor crew on the best ship, will likely sink it.

By the time Ben's business was sold, he and his team had not only achieved their targets but had significantly exceeded them. It had grown in value to £110m, far more than originally planned, and net profits had grown from £1m to £10m. A great business led by an exceptional CEO and Captain.

I have used this simple 'Captain's Voyage' framework with many businesses; from start-ups through to businesses with a turnover of several hundred million pounds. It has helped many CEOs and their teams achieve greater focus, pace and discipline in building value into their businesses. I believe it can help you too.

Becoming a successful, purpose-driven business leader and building a great, valuable business can be hard, but it doesn't need to be complex. Keep it simple and significant, and get sailing with FOCUS, PACE and DISCIPLINE. Surround yourself with good people, not only your staff, but experts, mentors and people who've sailed the journey before you. They will pick you up when you're down, celebrate with you when you succeed, and help you stay the course as you navigate your journey.

ABOUT THE AUTHOR

Keith Holdt's passion for creating highly-valuable, investor-worthy businesses, was sparked at aged six by his grandfather. A successful businessman himself, Keith was introduced to the world of building a business from scratch when he set eyes on the bustling furnace-making manufacturer which began in his grandfather's garage. It was the biggest of its kind in South Africa.

Of the many lessons picked up from his grandfather, the one that resonated most, was how he followed his dream, had a plan, and turned it into a highly successful business venture. There was a focus on accountability, leadership, and discipline, but also on advice and counsel. And so the maiden voyage of many in Keith's successful career, was mapped out.

Over the course of his international career, Keith has been on every side of the table and has helped businesses deliver over £1 billion of shareholder returns. The experience has provided him with invaluable insight and understanding into what investors are looking for in a CEO, and how to become that CEO for investors. Having been in the trenches both as a Chairman and CEO, he understands the pain leaders go through when times are tough, and also the joy of victory when there is success.

At the heart of every business is the team, and at the head of the team is the CEO. Keith recognised that CEOs who are heralded for their work, are the same CEOs struggling under pressure from investors, with few having the right investor mindset, confidence, focus, pace and discipline needed to achieve and exceed their business plans.

With this in mind he founded Equity Impact Partners, to support and inspire ambitious business leaders and their teams. Together, they build and deliver powerful equity stories that are compelling for investors, igniting what they do to create powerful, highly valuable businesses of impact and influence.

Keith continues to pioneer the movement towards supporting CEOs as they embark on their journey to build highly successful businesses. His passion, support and knowledge provide invaluable insights, as he guides, directs and supports them using his expertise from every angle.

Keith loves the outdoors, whether it is diving off the African coast or walking in the hills. When he is not at home in Richmond, London, he likes nothing better than to be in his croft cottage on the banks of Loch Fyne in Scotland, close to the water and surrounded by the rugged beauty of the hills.

If I know two people, the number of possible connections in the network is 3. If there are just 10 people in the network the number of connections rises to 45. 14 becomes 91 separate connections. Ideas and connections spread fast and easily, without having to be enormous.

CHRIS MCKIBBIN

20 NETWORKS & THE COLLECTIVE BRAIN

The notion of the lone genius is an attractive one. From Leonardo Da Vinci to Albert Einstein to Ada Lovelace, society (and innovation circles in particular) fetishizes them and lauds their unmatchable talent, their unique knowledge. And of course, these folks had great talent in their underlying fields. However, their special sauce wasn't that they necessarily *knew* any more than their peers – it was really their ability to simultaneously hold different lenses to a problem and consider them differently.

Whilst not all of us can do that inside our individual brains, the same lenses are available to us. We just have to tap into collective, collaborative knowledge to enable it. And where do we find collective knowledge? Networks. Networks are the key to democratising knowledge.

To be clear from the outset, this chapter isn't really about how to network – there are lots of books dedicated to help you do that. Rather, I'd like to highlight some of the reasons networks are important for us; why they can be daunting for us to engage with (but needn't be); and dispel some of the myths surrounding them.

It is my belief that networks are the key to scaling knowledge to individual and collective benefit. To that end, I've included some references to this on the way through, and added a recommended set of books that have helped me.

WHERE IT ALL STARTED FOR ME

Two years in to my time at Capita, a large outsourcing and software company, I was introduced to the annual senior management conference as CHRIS – the Customer Hierarchy Relationship Information System (creativity was short the day we made that acronym up!) I represented Capita's investment in CRM. I was referred to as a signposter, an encyclopedia, even 'glue.' Technology solutions (even allowing for the fact it was some time ago) were expressly off the table. My boss at the time was clear – you will always get more out of a 5 minute phone call with someone than you ever will out of a database. If you don't know the right person to talk to, find someone who might and go and ask them.

Now, having been brought up in a family of lawyers, with the prebuilt determination that I too would become a lawyer in due course, personal knowledge was understood to equate to value. So it took me a while to get comfortable with how I was to be valuable to my colleagues. I wasn't necessarily the end source of information for them – *shouldn't I have been?* I certainly wasn't the expert in any one sector or domain – *did I have to be?*

But what I *was*, was curious and this curiosity led me to becoming well-connected, initially within the organisation, and then more broadly. My knowledge provided them with a fast, painless, (at times probably over-accessible) route to information they needed. I began to understand that you don't have to know it all to be valuable. However, if you don't know it, try and know someone who does. My boss was (and remains) right.

All this means I've spent much of my professional career studying, building or helping facilitate successful networks and collaborations.

3 VIEWPOINTS ON THE IMPORTANCE OF NETWORKS

SOCIETIES

It's inherently easier to understand our societies as networks than as hierarchies. Professor Sandy Pentland at MIT Connection Science[1] has dedicated over a decade of research to understanding how ideas flow through social networks of all shapes and sizes, and ultimately how this translates into how humans behave. The remarkable findings from his team's research show that there are predictable patterns in how networks behave. We're not as independent as we might think!

Setting aside the indignation we as individuals might be feeling at this revelation, the good news is that by appreciating this, we can establish means to tweak how our networks work for us and for societal good overall. Diversity and social learning – learning from others – are the keys. The more we and our societies' functions can connect with people with different skillsets, backgrounds, knowledge and lenses, the better and faster we can get to, not just good questions and good answers, but also good behaviours and good results. A simple (but complicated) example in the UK might be how we might secure good health for citizens. If we could reliably establish better idea flow – more effective networks – nationally across the National Health Service, the local trusts, social care bodies, local government and the private sector, we would clearly generate better outcomes.

ORGANISATIONS

Our traditional view of the workplace is a monolith of full-time workers. We have an embedded, industrialisation-era view that all workers should be permanent and that working hours and the place of work should be fixed. It makes for simple (or at least simpler) classical, line-of-sight management and planning; all seemingly very efficient.

However, that whole world view continues to be challenged by factors including (but not limited to), the ramifications of the Covid pandemic, a shrinking away from globalism towards nationalism, and the impacts of connectivity and technology.

So, what if we looked at the workforce as a network of networks, rather than a hierarchy? This ecosystem would be made up of the skills and knowledge found within teams of permanent and part-time workers, contractors, service providers, strategic partners, academia, remote workers – and (even!) customers.

In 1989, Charles Handy, a management theorist, wrote an extraordinarily prescient book called The Age of Unreason[2]. In it, he describes what he called the 'Shamrock Organisation.' His thesis outlined a future of how organisations and work would be structured that was hard to imagine at the time, but one that is coming into focus clearly today.

It would be made up of three types of workers: the three leaves of this eponymous shamrock:

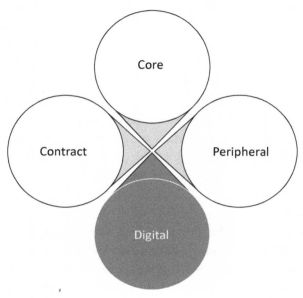

Handy's network comprised:

1. The Core – a small number of permanent executives and professionals who conceived new products or services, maintained the culture, and set the strategic direction.
2. Contractors – a diverse group of contractors and consultants who built the products or developed the services through a series of flexibly staffed projects.
3. Peripherals – the transient contingent workforce used as needed to support the projects or to provide an on-demand source of skills as needs waxed and waned.

Because I'm Irish, consider myself generally lucky these days, and have spent the past decade looking at automation technologies, I've added a fourth, new leaf – the Digital Workforce – to capture the rapidly evolving role of automation and AI technologies that increasingly perform or augment hitherto human roles.

The original definitions can be debated, where should flexible or part-time working be included etc., but in the overall, emerging paradigm, the network is the cohering theme. More work will be done in teams, and more focus will be placed on learning to lead teams, collaborate and negotiate, and work across many different functions, knowledge bases, and cultures. The concept of the individual contributor will disappear in favour of the team player. The appeal of the lone genius will be (at least) systematically dented.

INDIVIDUALS

If we continue this line of thinking, the kind of individuals that will grow in demand will have developed collaboration, communication and innovation skills; practices which leverage our very human need to socialise, share, and create, and which rely on relationships and connections to achieve success.

Porter Gale[3], the former CMO at Virgin America once quipped 'Your network is your net worth.' As well as being a neat book title, this assertion is borne out by research from Ronald S. Burt[4] at the Chicago Booth School of Business, whose studies have described a direct correlation between the scale and nature of an individual's networks, and measures of success.

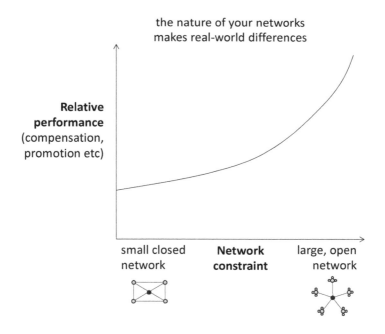

The more closed the network you find yourself in, the more likely you are to be limited to lower value work. Conversely, the more open your network is, the more likely you are to be paid more and to be promoted more often. Now, it must be recognised that financial success is not the be all and end all – it is only one measure of one type of success. For me, though, it feels intuitive that more open, diverse connections also result in other, more personal measures of success as well.

3 HEADWINDS

Getting yourself or your organisation involved in networks, or trying to set them up, isn't always straightforward. It requires dedication and, more often than not, a sustained mindset shift. Some of these shifts are subtle and personal and can be quite challenging to resolve.

'Networking is a contact sport' – Anon

I love contact sports. I played rugby at an U19 International World Cup. But I'm also a fully paid-up extroverted introvert. I can't think of anything more horrifying than going into a room full of people with the prescribed aim of getting 20 business cards. Networking as an idea is too often promoted as an in your face, meet everyone, 'work the room,' extract value from the people you meet, kind of thing. It makes my blood run cold.

Realising that building a good network is really a result of being curious, and helping further others curiosity, was a watershed for me. It blew that horror away. I was curious about other people, their areas of expertise, about areas of overlap and collaboration. I was curious how I could help other people feed their interests. That was the contact I was interested in. Networking – the amassing of a vast rolodex of contacts – was not the end itself.

It was a win-win. I could indulge my curiosity and my appetite to learn, increase my sources of inspiration and open up avenues of conversation that might or might not lead anywhere. The pressure valve was released.

'In the beginner's mind there are many possibilities, but in the expert's there are few.'[5]

The more expertise we think we have, the more closed we tend to be toward new ideas. Confirmation bias – perhaps our strongest cognitive bias – makes intuitive but perverse sense: if I know the answer, then why bother revisiting options or the logic by which I arrived at our current answer?

This intellectual introversion can also be exacerbated in times of stress. With the challenges presented by the Covid pandemic, we've watched this play out at all levels. Nations pulling up economic and political drawbridges, organisations bunkering down and hoping that their existing assets and business model will be good enough to survive, individuals coping however they can – perhaps by forcing all the pressure onto themselves in pursuit of that lone genius idea that will bring them security. These vicious cycles can be hard to pull ourselves and our organisations out of.

Collaborating in networks is an exceptional means to challenge status quo expert thinking. Naïve questions from peers or experts in other fields cannot be underestimated as a means of exploration! If we can extract ourselves from our own egos – constrained and enabled as they are by everything else that forms us – we can free ourselves to learn and better address problems afresh.

'I'm going to get caught out any day now...'[6]

Pulling in directly the opposite way from perceived expertise is imposter syndrome – a perception that we aren't really expert (or expert enough) to contribute.

Growing up in Northern Ireland, self-deprecation was a baked in way of life. It simply didn't do to stick your head over the parapet and be brash and braying. Coming across to University in Nottingham I met lots of seemingly impossibly self-confident peers. I simply shrank into myself. I felt this keenly through my career, though I tried to hide it – sometimes effectively, sometimes not – and never more so than when I decided to leave the comfort of my corporate job to try my hand at something different.

For the 5 years previous I'd led on engaging with the ecosystem of start-ups, scaling companies and global giants that were developing emerging technologies. Every day I met with smart, driven people who had the self-belief to risk it all and bet on themselves and their ideas, which was inspiring – and challenging. Steadily I convinced myself I didn't really deserve to have got where I was, in the face of these folks risking it all.

As an independent consultant, I would have the opportunity to strip everything away and prove to myself that I was able to plough my own furrow. Despite some success to date, the feeling has never really gone away! This feeling – as I discovered meeting other independent consultants – isn't uncommon. In fact it's pretty prevalent. Amongst its impacts, it can also inhibit our willingness to join in conversations, put ourselves in front of other people, or surround ourselves with differently-skilled folks.

The (ongoing) trick is to get comfortable with being uncomfortable, and to remember that people are generally supportive of genuine, authentic engagement.

3 MYTHS ABOUT NETWORKS

NETWORKS DON'T HAVE TO BE HUGE TO BE EFFECTIVE

Much like compound interest, networks don't have to comprise hundreds of contacts to generate useful results. The easiest way to see this is to visualise it as below:

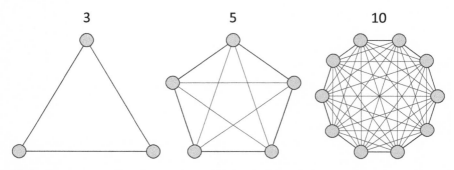

If I know two people, the number of possible connections in the network is 3. If there are just 10 people in the network the number of connections rises to 45. 14 becomes 91 separate connections. Ideas and connections spread fast and easily, without having to be enormous.

Clearly, the impact of the network depends not only on the number of participants, but also their diversity. The power of these networks can be greatly enhanced by deliberately focussing on the diversity of thought within them (see Chris Paton's Chapter 15). To illustrate with an example: Aviva regularly ran hackathons, including underwriters, developers and team leaders, to co-develop an app for commercial underwriters. Underwriters were invited to pitch ideas, and those shortlisted were teamed with a developer. Each short-listed idea was built and went live with a prize given to the winner as judged by a panel. All of this led to a win/win/win - diversity of ideas by deliberately drawing together focussed networks of skills; genuine engagement of front-line teams/users; and new, useful functionality delivered.

NETWORKS DON'T HAVE TO TAKE DECADES TO BUILD TO BE EFFECTIVE

My grandmother was fond of the saying 'needs must when the devil drives.' It's a plainer-speaking version of the 'necessity is the mother of invention' quote many of us will be familiar with.

An associate of mine is a consultant actuary. As an independent consultant, he struggled to find a way to keep up his mandatory professional CPD hours. So he decided to set up a network to enable him and his fellow independent contractors to connect and share quality, curated content that would allow them to keep up their credits, and also facilitate peer support.

Beginning just 4 years ago, with meetings in central London after work, the Network of Consulting Actuaries has now grown from scratch to over 2,000 members globally. Engagement is genuinely incredible, with 350-400 people tuning in to their regular webinars. It's also a great example of the classic network effect described above: the more people join, the greater the net value to the members.

NETWORKS DON'T HAVE TO 'BELONG' TO YOU TO BE EFFECTIVE

Isaac Newton famously said, 'If I have seen further than others, it is by standing on the shoulders of giants.' It is often easier, faster and more effective to tap into prebuilt collective support, as well as (or instead of) replicating it yourself – as seen in the entire services and software industries.

As above, networks already exist in many specialist fields. One of the big realisations that has dawned on organisations large and small, is that the pace of change is now too great for them to own all parts of the value chain. Accelerators for start-ups, academic research partnerships, health and science networks, professional accrediting bodies, have all been established with the sole aim of facilitating connections with partners to that network's specific area of expertise.

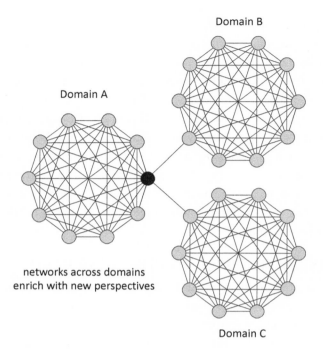

Domain B

Domain A

Domain C

networks across domains
enrich with new perspectives

As an example, The Camelot Network[7] was originally formed to address a fundamental need many independent consultants have; the need to feel part of something, the desire to help others and to learn. It has grown from 0 to almost 200 independent consultants in two years. Being comprised of former CIOs and COOs, Heads of Data Science and Transformation Directors, it is now an enviable means to learn and engage with the Insurance market in the UK by standing on the shoulders of senior, seasoned folks.

WHERE IT'S ALL GOING

We started this chapter with a reflection on democratising knowledge. Social and collaboration tools are part of this, of course, but there is now software that can help capture and scale expert human knowledge. Not by coincidence, these tools are designed as knowledge graphs, which both visually resemble and technically operate just like networks with relationships between nodes/members. These will have a seismic effect on professional services and will be a key part in the lucky-shamrock-shaped organisation of the future.

Someone much cleverer than me said of other recent advances in machine learning and AI, that, 'We are midwife to a new form of intelligence.' I would argue the same is true of networks. Despite not being a new concept, very few organisations have truly changed shape or made best use of the collective brainpower of their own people. In a world of work that is shifting away from a traditional 9-5, five days a week sole job, we all need to identify and understand the power of networks beyond company borders – and our own – and involve and leverage them.

It's the fastest way we have to get to better questions, and the fastest way to better answers.

BOOKS I'VE FOUND USEFUL, INTERESTING AND ACCESSIBLE:
Linked – Albert Laszlo Barabasi
Social Physics – Prof. Alex 'Sandy' Pentland
The Age of Unreason – Charles Handy
Range – David Epstein

ENDNOTES

1   https://www.media.mit.edu/people/sandy/overview/

2   Charles Handy, The Age of Unreason.   Random House ISBN 0099548313

3   Porter Gale: Your Network is your Net Worth, Simon & Schuster 2013

4   Ronald S. Burt, Chicago Booth School of Business, 2019

5   Shunryu Suzuki – Zen Mind, Beginner's Mind: Informal Talks on Zen Meditation and Practice

6   Me. Most days.

7   https://thecamelotnetwork.com/

ABOUT THE AUTHOR

At his heart, Chris is a curious soul who grew up late.

A Northern Irish self-confessed extroverted introvert, he slowly realised that working in support of others and being a network 'glue' brought both personal and professional satisfaction. This, and early achievements in team sports, seated in him the belief that diverse perspectives and collaboration usually lead to better outcomes.

This service / collaboration mentality has served him well in results-oriented but loosely-specified environments, where success depends on getting things done, from ideas to execution to scaling. Having built innovation and technology ecosystem strategies within, and for, large Corporates, through to niche innovation brokers, clients, academia, accelerators and start/scale-ups, he has spent a lot of his life convincing smart, strong-minded people that the answers to their questions aren't always inside the room.

In part, he founded his current company www.LogicLayer.co.uk in response to an argument about the value of individual knowledge with his father (a lawyer). Combined with his interest in emerging technologies, he now helps organisations grow, control and deliver better outcomes. By pulling out business logic and expert knowledge buried in software applications, processes and colleagues' heads, he creates tangible Decisioning Assets that can be used, re-used and evolved across the organisation.

Equally fascinating to him are the social and corporate consequences of these technologies - and maybe one day he'll win that argument!

Sport and teams are hugely important to Chris. He played International U19-level Rugby at the FIRA World Cup; played Cricket for Ireland and Ulster Schools; was President of the Nottingham University Cricket Club; and is a current Playing Member of the Marylebone Cricket Club (MCC). Latterly he was Chair of a local cricket club, rebuilding the youth section from 0 to 50+ children and securing multi-thousand pound grants for equipment and clubhouse refurbishment.

His wonderful blended family of 4 children and Céline, are the rock on which he leans daily. They have given him the self-confidence to contribute to this book alongside a phenomenal cadre of leaders.

https://www.linkedin.com/in/chrismck/

PROCEEDS FROM THIS BOOK WILL BE DONATED TO THE FOLLOWING CHARITIES:

https://www.shelter.org.uk/

https://www.ssafa.org.uk/

https://cancerfundforchildren.com/

samten

https://www.samten.co/